Microsoft

Making

Better

B U S I N E S S

I_n_t_e_l_l_i_g_e_n_c_e >>

Decisions

Faster

Elizabeth Vitt
Michael Luckevich
Stacia Misner

PUBLISHED BY
Microsoft Press
A Division of Microsoft Corporation
One Microsoft Way
Redmond, Washington 98052-6399

Library of Congress Cataloging-in-Publication Data
Vitt, Elizabeth.
    Business Intelligence : Making Better Decisions Faster / Elizabeth Vitt, Michael Luckevich.
       p. cm.
    Includes index.
    ISBN 0-7356-1627-2
    1. Business intelligence.   2. Decision support systems.   3. Management information
systems.   4. Information technology--Management.   I. Luckevich, Michael.   II. Title.

    HD38.7 .L83 2002
    658.4'038'011--dc21   2001057976

Printed and bound in the United States of America.

1 2 3 4 5 6 7 8 9   QWT   7 6 5 4 3 2

Distributed in Canada by Penguin Books Canada Limited.

A CIP catalogue record for this book is available from the British Library.

Microsoft Press books are available through booksellers and distributors worldwide. For further information about international editions, contact your local Microsoft Corporation office or contact Microsoft Press International directly at fax (425) 936-7329. Visit our Web site at www.microsoft.com/mspress. Send comments to *mspinput@microsoft.com*.

Acquisitions Editor: Alex Blanton
Project Editor: Jenny Moss Benson

Body Part No. X08-41933

Contents

About the Authors

Elizabeth Vitt

Elizabeth Vitt, a Manager at Aspirity, has six years of business development, project management, consulting, and training experience in business intelligence. Her industry experience includes implementations in retail, manufacturing, and health care. She has specialized expertise as an educator in data warehousing design and implementation and is an author of the *Microsoft Official Curriculum* (MOC) for Microsoft's business intelligence product offerings. Elizabeth is also a frequent speaker at Microsoft SQL Server conferences worldwide. Elizabeth earned a bachelor of science degree in environmental engineering from Northwestern University, Evanston, Illinois. She resides in Kirkland, Washington.

Michael Luckevich

Michael Luckevich, the Chief Executive Officer of Aspirity, has 18 years of information technology and business intelligence experience. Michael has extensive experience in the architecture, design, development, and implementation of complex business intelligence solutions. He frequently teaches classes and offers seminars on various topics relating to business intelligence, data warehousing, and OLAP technologies. Michael is a graduate of the University of Waterloo Faculty of Mathematics and resides in Bellevue, Washington, with his wife, Diana, and two children.

Stacia Misner

Stacia Misner, a Manager at Aspirity, has 17 years' experience as an information technology professional, educator, and consultant, focusing on business intelligence and decision support systems for many Fortune 500 companies. Stacia's industry experience includes implementations in accounting, retail, legal, insurance, automotive, agriculture, manufacturing, telecommunications, and health care. She also has specialized experience in developing business intelligence solution methodologies. Stacia currently resides in Lacey, Washington, with her husband, Gerry.

Contributing Authors

Aspirity is a professional services firm specializing in education and consulting related to business intelligence and associated technologies. With headquarters in Bellevue, Washington, Aspirity also has offices in Chicago and New York.

Hilary Feier, the President and Chief Operating Officer of Aspirity, has more than 10 years of consulting, training, project management, and executive experience in business intelligence. Hilary is a coauthor of the *Microsoft Official Curriculum* (MOC) for Microsoft's business intelligence product offerings and is a frequent speaker at SQL Server conferences. She received a bachelor of arts degree in computer science from Brown University and a masters in business administration degree from the University of California, Berkeley, Haas School of Business. Hilary resides with her husband, Frank, in Kirkland, Washington.

Rand Heer, a member of Aspirity's Board of Directors, has more than 25 years' experience as the financial officer and chief executive of manufacturing, high-tech, and training businesses. He is currently President of Alight Business Technologies, a software company. As President of OLAP Train, he managed the development of the *Microsoft Official Curriculum* (MOC) for Microsoft's business intelligence product offerings. He earned a bachelor of arts degree in political science from the University of California, Riverside, California, and a masters in business administration degree from Harvard Business School. Rand resides with his wife, Valerie, in Kelsey, California.

Reed Jacobson, a Manager at Aspirity, has 20 years of information technology and business intelligence experience. Reed is the author of *Microsoft SQL Server 2000 Analysis Services Step by Step* and *Microsoft Excel Visual Basic for Applications Step by Step,* among other books. He has also developed the *Microsoft Official Curriculum* (MOC) for Microsoft's business intelligence product offerings as well as CD-ROM training on Microsoft Office products. Reed has given presentations around the world on Office, Microsoft Visual Basic, and SQL Server Analysis Services. Reed earned a bachelor of arts degree in Japanese and linguistics from Brigham Young University and a masters in business administration degree from the Marriott School of Management at Brigham Young University. Reed resides in Seattle, Washington.

Foreword

Business intelligence has never been more important. Fortunately, it has never been so easy to implement and use business intelligence (BI) systems. These are sweeping statements. Allow me to explain.

I recently read about a start-up software vendor that received tens of millions of dollars in venture capital. It was a flashback for me. Since 1996, I have worked at Microsoft. My friends at dot-com companies thought Microsoft was so square with our focus on profits, bottom-line growth, and other old-fashioned measures. Well...we're all squares now!

The demand for profits, the contracting economy, increasing competition, and savvy customers all require corporations and organizations to make the best decisions possible. I maintain that the company with the best employees—employees who make correct and timely decisions—wins. But how do you ensure that employees, at every level of an organization, make the best decisions they can? This is the role of business intelligence. When done right, business intelligence brings tools and data to every employee, in a format each can use, on a device each has, when each needs it.

Customers, be they consumers or business partners, have choices. They have access to information, essentially in real time, that helps them make educated product and service selections. I grew up as a Bell-baby, that is, both of my parents worked for the telephone company. In the 1960s no one imagined that consumers could (or would) pick their telephone service provider (or even buy their own phones!). Now, in some states, we have our choice of electric utilities. The information that consumers have enables them to make better decisions. *What are you doing to enable your employees to make better decisions?*

The Internet, even in the face of the dot-com debacle, is a very real and permanent facet of today's business world. It forces a real-time aspect to decision making, to the point of requiring that some decisions be made automatically. Even without the real-time component, the Internet allows customers to evaluate more choices, faster than ever before. *What are you doing to allow your employees to keep pace?*

As companies expand across geographic and product boundaries, span of control increasingly becomes an issue. Sharing best practices becomes harder. Regional differences become important. Decisions made locally, sometimes in the presence of the customer, are more relevant and more immediate. *How are you supporting local decision makers?*

In the 1980s and the 1990s, corporations invested massive amounts in operational systems. Many companies made a fresh round of investments in anticipation of Y2K. These operational systems are churning daily, generating the masses of data needed to support insightful business analysis—the key to developing breakthrough business strategies. *What are you doing to unlock and use the data stored in operational systems?*

A first premise is that BI systems of various forms are the answers to each of these challenges. Business intelligence is one of the few forms of sustainable competitive advantage left. Why? Deep down, any two well-funded competitors in a market have near equal access to capital, technology, market research, customer data, and distribution. People and the quality of decisions that they make are the primary competitive differentiators in the Information Age. The proprietary *implementation* of standard BI components is the key to sustaining long-term competitive advantage.

My second premise is that it has never been easier to implement and use BI systems. Numerous trends are responsible. The first, and the one I am most proud of, is that BI software is more accessible than ever. By accessible I mean software that is easy and cost-effective to acquire, install, populate (with data and rules), deploy, and use. Microsoft software, including Microsoft SQL Server 2000 and Microsoft Office, has played a key role in driving this trend.

There was a time when every IT department was staffed with application programmers, often working in COBOL. Business applications were idiosyncratic to individual businesses. Any attempt to provide business intelligence on top of operational systems was met by the frustration of pulling data from numerous systems. At a time when companies struggled to integrate operational systems, BI people were completely disadvantaged. Many of those large IT departments have shrunk as companies adopt packaged enterprise resource planning (ERP) systems and other business applications. The nascent and struggling trend toward application service providers (ASPs) furthers this trend. As business applications become more standardized, it becomes easier to implement BI systems.

While the Internet creates a new set of challenges to business, it also opens up opportunity for BI systems. Internet protocols such as Extensible Markup Language (XML) and others are leading to an era of commodity access to data. Effective decision making often requires data from outside the organization. This might be partner and customer data or third-party data from governments or research organizations. In both cases, standard formats reduce yet another barrier for the BI implementer.

For companies that do business over the Internet, we have access to a new source of data: direct evidence of consumer behavior. A company I worked for years ago had a partner company that built helmets that tracked eye movements. They sought volunteer shoppers in supermarkets to wear the helmets. They could, in theory, track consumer reactions to packaging, placement, and other variables. It never worked. Consumers who view Web pages and buy or don't buy are giving us the data we always wanted but could not cheaply acquire.

Finally toward this trend I want to brag a little more about the Microsoft BI platform. Until SQL Server 7.0, OLAP and other BI technologies were considered expensive and esoteric. Our goal with the Microsoft BI platform was, and is, to make the software affordable and implementable by organizations of any size, including small groups inside very large corporations. I think we have met that goal, even as we invest to push the phenomenon even further.

So you need business intelligence and it is easier to implement than ever before. But as a business decision maker, what can you do? The answer is simple—read this book!

The technical features of the Microsoft BI platform are well documented in other books. This book really addresses the business decision maker and shows why you, as a business decision maker, should use business intelligence in the first place. In Chapter 1, "Understanding Business Intelligence," the authors carefully cover the basics of what you need to know (and might be afraid to ask) before embarking on a BI project: how business intelligence is defined, how and why it is used in an organization, and the features that most BI solutions share. Chapter 3, "Defining BI Technologies," guides you through the technical details of business intelligence.

A highlight of this book is the case studies in Part 2. The authors detail how leaders in financial, manufacturing, and retail companies successfully implemented BI solutions and reaped benefits. They explain the business challenges, the tools and strategies used, why decisions were made, and so forth. Perhaps you will recognize some of your organization's own challenges in this section.

In Part III the authors present a roadmap for creating a BI success story. Careful attention is paid in how to implement a BI solution. In Chapter 9, "Identifying BI Opportunities," the authors show you how to identify and evaluate specific opportunities where you can use business intelligence to improve the quality of corporate decision making. In Chapter 10, "Implementing a BI Solution," they offer practical advice about what decisions you will need to make to undertake a BI solution and what best practices will make sure that your BI solution is successful.

Aspirity has been a true friend of Analysis Services and the Microsoft SQL BI team for years. These two companies have worked together on numerous projects. The SQL Server BI team at Microsoft started working with Aspirity several years ago when Corey Salka, one of our managers, engaged Aspirity founder Tom Chester to develop sample code and databases for our emerging OLAP server. Over time the relationship both deepened and broadened. The Microsoft team relies on Aspirity for training and implementation services. The Aspirity team has had direct input into the evolution and development of Analysis Services. I have crossed paths with Hilary Feier and other Aspirity founders so often that I often forget that they are not Microsoft employees!

Liz, Michael, and Stacia are seasoned BI practitioners. Aspirity is a leader in BI consulting and training, with deep experience in the major BI technologies and database platforms, and these authors demonstrate why Aspirity has been successful in all these businesses. They have worked with hundreds of customers and can relate those experiences to others in plain language. When you read this book, you are touching on more than 40 person-years of BI experience. I cannot think of a more qualified team to bring business intelligence into focus for a business audience.

Great corporations are adopting business intelligence to empower their employees to make great decisions. IT teams are not oblivious to business intelligence. The decision makers in your organization are not unaware of business intelligence. This book will equip you to talk the talk so that they can walk the walk.

Bill Baker
General Manager,
Microsoft SQL Server Business Intelligence

Introduction

Rapid advances in economic globalization and information technology have forced many organizations to anticipate and respond to increasing volatility and competitive pressures. Achieving a position of competitive advantage requires companies to quickly identify market opportunities and take advantage of them in a fast and effective manner. More and more organizations are realizing that becoming increasingly rich in data does not necessarily result in a better understanding of their markets or improvements in operational performance. Business intelligence is the buzzword most popularly used to characterize those products and approaches aimed at making this desired result a reality.

In the past decade many books have treated business intelligence primarily as a technical topic, without paying much attention to motivations for superior business intelligence, such as securing competitive advantage, improving operational efficiency, increasing profitability—in short, maximizing shareholder value. *Business Intelligence: Making Better Decisions Faster* puts the business back into business intelligence by offering practical advice and real-world success stories that demonstrate how business intelligence can help organizations make better decisions faster.

Our Assumptions About You

This book is for business decision makers who want to learn what business intelligence (BI) means, what BI solutions look like, and how to take advantage of BI opportunities in their organization. It is also an excellent resource for technology professionals who already understand the wonders of BI technology but seek the words and anecdotes to explain to a nontechnical audience how these technologies benefit the business.

To help demonstrate BI concepts for the business audience, we provide several examples throughout the book that address common business problems in sales, marketing, operations, human resources, finance, and other functional areas. The more background you have in these areas, the more meaningful these examples will be. We also present technical BI terms in simple, jargon-free language, without burdening you with layers of technical details.

Organization of the Book

This book has been written to accomplish the following goals: (1) explain what business intelligence can offer to your organization; (2) demonstrate how business intelligence is used in the real world; and (3) provide an action plan for identifying and acting on the BI opportunities that exist in your organization. To this end, this book has been divided into three parts:

- Part I, "Business Intelligence Foundations," defines business intelligence and describes its role in the effective management of an organization. This part explains the business, technical, and human components of business intelligence and sets the stage for the case studies in Part II.

- Part II, "Business Intelligence Case Studies," presents five real-world BI success stories—Audi AG, Cascade Designs, CompUSA, Disco SA, and the Frank Russell Company—to illustrate different applications of business intelligence. This part presents how each of these companies applied business intelligence to improve the quality of corporate decision making and successfully overcome common business problems.

- Part III, "A Business Intelligence Roadmap," describes a framework and process for identifying, evaluating, and acting on specific BI opportunities in your organization. We present several guidelines to help you participate in the implementation of a BI solution.

To help you get your BI solution up and running quickly, the appendix of the book presents the BI technologies and tools available from Microsoft Corporation.

Acknowledgments

This book has been a collaborative effort—assembling the experiences, visions, and perspectives of the entire Aspirity team. We thank the industry visionaries in business intelligence and data warehousing for their participation and insights during the development of the book: among these are Bill Baker of Microsoft; Nigel Pendse of *The OLAP Report;* Claudia Imhoff of

Intelligent Solutions, Inc.; Joe Nicholson of Informatica; Dan Bulos of Symmetry Corporation; and Rick Hall of G4 Analytics.

The authors extend a special thank-you to the five companies that were willing to share their real-life experiences and achievements in business intelligence as well as those people who were instrumental in collecting the case study information.

- *Audi AG*—Martin Arndt and Heinz Braun of Audi AG; Helmut Knappe and Andreas Niegel of dc soft GmbH

- *Cascade Designs*—Lee Fromson and Ken Meidell of Cascade Designs

- *CompUSA*—Steve Ellison, Anna Halbert, Dennis Naherny, Landon West, and Cathy Witt of CompUSA; Donna Conner, Kim Foster, Regina Rafraf, and Darrell Becker of Microsoft Corporation, Redmond, Washington

- *Disco SA*—Horacio Diaz and Carlos Ocaranza of Disco SA; Hernan Gazzo, Adrian Mourelos, and Pablo Fondevila of Microsoft Buenos Aires

- *The Frank Russell Company*—Eric Espinal, Rod Greenshields, Matt Knox, and Thomas Morton of the Frank Russell Company

We also recognize the people who contributed to the successful production of this book. We could not have done it without you! We thank Alex Blanton and Jenny Moss Benson of Microsoft Press for their never-ending patience and help in driving this project to completion. We thank Brian Biglin of Microsoft Corporation for his development of the appendix and his coordination of the book's review. We also thank the following people from Microsoft Corporation for their excellent insight and continued support throughout the entire project: Francois Ajenstat, Thierry D'hers, John Eng, Euan Garden, Don Peterson, and Frank Rossi.

On a personal note, special thanks to Rosanne Luckevich, who inspired the prologue; Reed Jacobson for his continued inspiration and enthusiasm; Rand Heer of OLAP Train, who came to the rescue more than once; and Hilary Feier for her gifted and critical editing and willingness to offer frank and honest opinions even in the wee hours of the morning.

Finally, thanks to our colleagues at Aspirity for their assistance, patience, and faith in the authors.

Business Intelligence Foundations

In the first part of *Business Intelligence: Making Better Decisions Faster,* we lay some very important foundations for the executive, the manager, or the analyst who wants to learn what business intelligence is and what value it offers to the organization.

As a prologue to Chapter 1, we start with a short story about a woman named Lisa who finds herself in a bind. She wants to make a mark at Fabrikam, the company for whom she works, but the path to success is quite bumpy until she starts using business intelligence to overcome some difficult problems. The story illustrates the main message of Chapter 1, "Understanding Business Intelligence," that business intelligence is an attitude toward problem solving. The process starts with analysis, which leads to insight, action, and then measurement of the results. In this chapter we also look at the enablers of business intelligence—how technology, people, and culture come together to facilitate business intelligence.

Chapter 2, "Bridging the Analysis Gap," examines how systems designed for business intelligence transform the mountains of raw data within an organization into valuable information that is understandable and useful to decision makers. We describe the power of multidimensional analysis and discuss the *top-down, slice and dice* approach that decision makers use to analyze business problems. We explain how technologies optimized to support this form of business analysis can provide answers to ad hoc lines of questioning almost as quickly as the questions occur, thus providing a quantum breakthrough in the quality of business analysis— something we call *analysis at the speed of thought.*

Chapter 3, "Defining BI Technologies," provides a detailed discussion of the essential structures and technologies used to construct business intelligence systems. While this chapter contains technical information, it is presented in an easy-to-read format to help business decision makers understand where data comes from, where data is stored, how data is integrated, and how data gets into the hands of business users.

Prologue

The Mystery on Lovesick Lake

By the time she noticed, it was too late. Her four-year-old half-ton pickup gave a resounding "thunk" as the right front tire slammed into a pothole. She gripped the steering wheel with both hands and eased up on the accelerator. Hitting a pothole at 100 feet per second is dangerous in any vehicle, much less an aging truck.

Lisa Jacobson checked the clock and did a quick mental calculation. The gift shop wouldn't open for two hours. She had plenty of time. She slowed down. She'd been zipping along out of habit rather than necessity.

Lisa reflected on the irony of having plenty of time this morning. The greater truth was that she was completely out of time. Four months earlier she was the hero at Fabrikam, the second largest wholesaler of specialty gift and novelty items in Canada. Now she was fighting to keep her job. She had exactly two weeks before the start of a long July weekend. If sales didn't show a major improvement after this weekend, she was toast, and her job as director of imports would be an embarrassment on her resume rather than a source of pride. Her biggest campaign ever was on the brink of failure. The thought of screwing up so badly infuriated her.

She took a deep cleansing breath and tried to relax. She had wasted five weeks because of her own stubbornness, hanging onto a bad model of how this campaign should be run. Worse still, she had successfully managed to get everyone else, including Charlie, her boss, and Roger, the chief executive officer (CEO), to buy into the model. She had done her job too well. She was too persuasive about something that now looked not just wrong but stupid. The investment in inventory and promotion costs for the Peruvian doll campaign was over half a million dollars. Another half million was at risk from the channel expansion.

She needed answers right now. Though she had never visited the store before, Lisa was certain that the key answers could be found this morning at the gift shop on Lovesick Lake in Peterville. "Stay calm, think clearly," she murmured to herself. "You *will* solve the mystery of Store 9841." Lecturing to herself sometimes worked.

The sign at the entrance to town showed *Township of Peterville, Population 72,000.* The highway widened and was banked by gas stations and restaurants on both sides. She thought about pulling over for breakfast. She could also go over the numbers one more time.

Lisa pulled into a restaurant that had no advertising other than a big red neon sign that said "DINER." She focused a lot on branding in her job. She found it amusing that in choosing a restaurant in a new town, she consistently ignored the fancy signage and chain images and looked instead for the place with the fullest parking lot. She wondered if anyone ever studied parking lot metrics.

Entering the diner, she was conscious of the waitress staring at her faded jeans. A university sweatshirt and old tennis shoes completed her attire—not her normal business suit for a customer visit. This was her disguise for snooping around incognito. Lisa then realized that it wasn't her jeans. The waitress was focusing on her bulging laptop carrying case.

"You'll be wanting one of our booths with Internet access," the waitress said as she led Lisa to a booth near the back. "I'll be back in a minute with the coffee."

Lisa slid into the booth and snapped open the laptop. She pulled out a well-scribbled notepad and flipped to a clean page. At the top she wrote, "Distributor 9841: Lovesick." She then double-clicked an icon on her desktop and starting drilling into the database structure that opened up. This was the Fabrikam store database that she had refreshed from her apartment early this morning. Four clicks and she was at the complete profile, inventory, and sales history for store 9841. She already knew which store record to drill into.

* * *

Fabrikam was well known in the trade, but that was it. While sales were close to $200 million per year, the company was largely invisible to end customers. Specialty gift retailing is a fragmented industry, with most outlets being single stores owned and operated by sole proprietors. Gift shoppers are typically searching for something unusual, so individual stores with their aura of uniqueness have some advantage over retail chains, where consumers expect to see similar merchandise from one outlet to another.

But individual store operators, like Linda Mitchell who owned the gift shop at Lovesick Lake, lack the economies of scale and access to overseas manufacturers that larger chains enjoy, which is what Fabrikam provided. By delivering a wide range of products to a large number of gift shops, Fabrikam had the buying power and could deal directly with the manufacturers, most of whom were overseas. Fabrikam's catalog listed over 400 items being sold in 350 stores in Ontario and Quebec—the two largest markets in Canada.

Lisa had worked for Fabrikam for five years. She joined Fabrikam after completing her MBA. A fast rising star, she had moved from merchandising analyst to director of imports in just three years. Lisa had so improved the process of getting products through the maze of government import regulations that what had been a five-month ordeal was now a five-week systematic process. Overseas manufacturers loved Fabrikam, and especially Lisa, because their products got onto store shelves faster than with other distributors. Many dangled offers of deep price cuts if Fabrikam stepped up volumes. With distribution restricted to Ontario and Quebec, however, it was tough to make the business case for higher quantity purchases. So that's when Lisa went on her mission to change the way Fabrikam looked at its business.

Sixty percent of Fabrikam's volume came from imported goods. The company incurred high fixed costs in product research and infrastructure to support its import purchasing. Because Fabrikam distributed to only two of ten provinces in Canada, Lisa saw her opening. Fabrikam should expand to other provinces because of the leverage of higher purchase volumes and broader coverage of fixed costs. She acknowledged that expansion would involve challenges in geography, logistics, regional preferences, language, and local government regulations, but these were surmountable if people would just embrace the idea and focus on how to make it work.

The first showdown came in September when Lisa's boss, Charlie Anderson, blocked a proposal to distribute a line of handmade Peruvian dolls throughout Canada. In the heat of the moment at a staff meeting, Lisa had lost her temper and accused Charlie of being afraid to take risks. Her exact words were, "You're a wimp, Charlie. Face it." The room became dead silent. A colleague finally joked, "Lisa, no real wimp would disagree with you."

She mumbled an apology, but Lisa knew that she had crossed a forbidden line. Roger Harui, Fabrikam's CEO, had also been at the meeting. He hadn't said a word.

The morning after the "wimp" meeting, as it was being called around the office, Lisa got a call from Roger asking her to join him for lunch. "Uh oh," thought Lisa. "This is the ax." As it turned out, that wasn't the case. Instead, Roger's agenda was to encourage Lisa to pursue the idea of expanding into other provinces. But the talk did include a reprimand.

"Lisa, your thinking is too insular," he started. "Your mental model of this—your understanding of how Fabrikam works and how this will affect us—is too oriented to your own job. With such a narrow focus, you'll never get the support from others that is needed for such a move as expanding into new geographies. Go back to the drawing board. Do a better, broader job. Find something really out of the box to wake us up. Give us some very good reasons for doing this thing."

Better a boot than an ax. Lisa then started digging into the corporate databases, nagging the information systems (IS) people for downloads and new reports, rejuvenating an abandoned compilation of store shelf utilization and margin statistics, and personally dumping data into spreadsheets and analyzing them.

The next presentation went better—a lot better. She started with the "core competency" pitch that everyone knew. "At Fabrikam, we understand the specialty gift market better than anyone else, and we know the real details of how to build a channel. That's a good foundation to start from. But, you know what? I don't think we really know how good we are at it."

Lisa starting walking the staff through a series of presentation slides, with some surprising insights. Finally, she came to the *coup de grace* slide (Figure P-1).

"To sum it up, our customers have some very, very good reasons to love Fabrikam. While we take only 26 percent of their shelf space, our products generate 41 percent of their sales and a whopping 51 percent of gross profits. These are statistics we can win with—it's called tooting the horn—that leads to the most difficult part of expanding—convincing new stores to sign up."

Chairs shuffled. Whispers. You could sense both excitement and skepticism. Then the questions started, and for the next hour Lisa defended her analysis and the numbers—the survey data, the underlying database structures, the allocation methods she used, and the sales projections. The IS director was the most challenging. He knew that Lisa had been working on something with all that data, and finally here it was. Nobody at Fabrikam

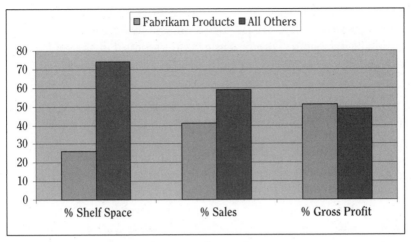

Figure P-1. *Fabrikam products vs. other products*

had done anything like this before. Usually financial analysts, not managers, crunched the numbers.

Roger leaned back, watched the action, and smiled. "No wimps here," he thought.

* * *

Lisa looked up from her laptop and poked at what was left of her scrambled eggs. Such a great presentation that was, and such a great response from Roger and everyone else. There was a whirlwind of real activity and commitment—new financial plans and forecasts, the hiring of two new regional directors, and opening new warehouse space in Vancouver. And, of course, the kickoff product line—the Peruvian dolls that Charlie had nixed at the wimp meeting.

Everything for the expansion had been executed according to plan, including spending a lot of up-front money for prospective new stores. Ninety new stores were signed up within three months. Then came the sales reports. "From hero to loser in three months," Lisa thought. The Peruvian dolls, their flagship product with the new distribution channel and a major campaign for the established stores, was selling at 19 percent of plan.

There were some explanations, such as weather, timing, and too steep a ramp, but most sounded like excuses. Finally, Lisa and her staff hit the road to find out what was really happening in the stores. They visited scores of new and old outlets. A few had not set up the point-of-purchase displays properly. At one store, the entire product shipment was still in the storage room. Lisa talked for hours with dozens of store owners, but she couldn't nail down anything concrete to explain the huge variance from the projections.

In the next weeks, sales crept up but very slowly. With great anxiety Lisa reviewed the results for the week that included a long vacation weekend at the end of May. Thirty-four percent of plan—maybe it was the weather. First two weeks of June—41 percent of plan; marginally better but still bad. Third week of June—25 percent of plan. The sky was falling, and the phone was ringing. There were now five calls from expansion stores wanting to ship back the dolls. Finally, Lisa was forced to look into the mirror. She had to accept what the data was telling her. Her Peruvian dolls were a dud.

Lisa glanced at the check, left a $10 bill, and headed for the restaurant exit. As she climbed into her truck, Lisa smiled broadly. She had rechecked the data at the restaurant, and it was clear. Whatever the answer, for better or worse, the mystery of the Peruvian dolls should be answered at the gift shop on Lovesick Lake.

* * *

In the parking lot of the shop, Lisa picked up a boxed doll that sat on the seat beside her. She studied the glossy beige color and the clear plastic front of the packaging she had designed. She examined the labeling in English and French. The packaging had been intentional. The neutral box color let the high-contrast colors of the doll costumes stand out. The high quality of the box added to the perceived value of the product.

Lisa removed the doll from the box and examined it. The craftsmanship was superb. The facial features were clearly painted. The hair was neatly braided and tied with ribbons. The care with which the costume had been sewn was evident. There was no better product on the market in the same price range. Was this really a dud or what?

Lisa stepped into the shop. A woman with shoulder-length salt and pepper hair, presumably Linda Mitchell, stood behind the sales counter and greeted Lisa warmly. Lisa nodded and smiled but said nothing. She turned to the interior and stood for a moment absorbing the scene. It took every bit of self-control to prevent her from racing through the shop searching for the dolls.

She wandered deeper into the displays, rapidly scanning the shelves at the five-foot level—the correct height for showing off the dolls. She expected to see a display of 48 dolls, 12 wide and 4 deep, with each doll standing neatly within its box staring out at the world. She did not expect to look down to table level and see a most delightful dollhouse. It was made of several shades of wood, all appearing to be unpainted but of such distinctive textures that the overall impression was remarkably lifelike.

She crouched down to study the dollhouse more closely—its superb craftsmanship and the detailing of the covered front porch that hosted a swing where one of the Peruvian dolls was placed. More dolls inhabited other rooms of the storybook house. Each was completely congruous, the fine details of their appearance matching that of the setting. One stood beside the fireplace somewhat askew. Without hesitation, she adjusted its position.

It was immediately clear to Lisa where she had erred. Her market testing had placed the actual doll into the hands of test customers. They had been able to examine the fine details at close range and feel the quality of the construction. The packaging, of which she was so proud, was preventing this in her specified displays. The dollhouse display showed the dolls in a far superior setting—really showing them off.

She read the small laminated placard that stood beside the dollhouse: "Unique handcrafted dollhouses available by special order. We ship anywhere. Lovesick Lake Dollhouse Company." The price was $299. Her mind raced through scenarios. Then she was startled by the owner who was standing beside her.

"May I help you?" asked Linda.

"You already have." Lisa's face beamed a great smile. "Let me introduce myself. I'm Lisa Jacobson. You must be Linda Mitchell."

* * *

The telephone rang, but Lisa didn't look up from her dinner of Chinese takeout. It was the fax line. Just as expected.

It had been a whirlwind of activity since her visit to Peterville—conferencing with her staff, rewriting the display recommendations, meeting with the dollhouse maker, driving hundreds of miles setting up displays, pitching store owners on the new approach. It came together quickly and cleanly.

The dollhouse maker was Linda Mitchell's brother, Harvey. His only channels were his sister's shop and word of mouth. When Lisa bought his inventory of five houses and ordered a hundred more, Harvey quit his job as a carpenter and started to work. The fax on Lisa's line was from Harvey, a signed distribution agreement between Fabrikam and the Lovesick Lake Dollhouse Company.

The best news was the impact on sales. It was like magic—every store where they placed a dollhouse showed an immediate improvement in doll sales. Even the stores where they just got them out of the box showed improvement. Overall sales of the Peruvian dolls were now 12 percent ahead of plan. Dollhouse sales were also supplementing the bottom line very nicely. "Thank-you very much," thought Lisa.

She thought back to her meeting with Charlie and Roger two weeks earlier. "You were two Peruvian doll cancellations away from getting canned," teased Charlie as he smiled broadly. "It would have been half a million down the toilet."

"I know, it was just that..." said Lisa.

"Lisa," Roger interrupted. "We want to know how you figured out about the dollhouses. You'd been plugging around in all that data, but there was nothing in the database about the dollhouses." Roger and Charlie looked at her with question marks on their faces.

"OK, guys," said Lisa. "A couple of nights before I went to Peterville, I was struck by a lightning bolt. I was asking the wrong question."

"And the wrong question was?" asked Charlie.

"I was asking what's going wrong?" answered Lisa. "I was looking at the problem upside down. Instead of focusing on what was wrong at many outlets, I needed to find some examples of what was going right at one or a few outlets, if there were any."

Lisa explained how she had studied all the standard sales reports, which included summaries by province, region, and district, plus listings of the top 10 and bottom 10 districts. There was no reporting by individual stores, however. The IS department used to print out these reports, but they were cancelled a year ago. As the company grew and the number of stores multiplied, nobody seemed interested in store-level data, except the field representatives who got special store reports for their districts.

Out of frustration, Lisa asked IS for a copy of the entire sales database with every sales transaction down to the store level for the previous 12 months, which she loaded in a multidimensional database on her laptop. She spent hours massaging the data, looking at variances and peculiarities. But nothing clear-cut jumped out until...

"Finally, I stumbled onto the right question, which was, 'Is anybody doing anything right?'"

Lisa continued: "By analyzing which stores were doing good as well as bad, I found there was only one store that had performed as expected more than two of the five weeks. That one store had performed as expected in all five weeks. It was obvious to me that they knew something about selling dolls that I did not. Here, I'll show you."

Lisa stopped, thought a second, and then flipped open her laptop. She double-clicked an icon and selected a saved view. There it was at the top of the list—the gift shop on Lovesick Lake (Table P-1), the only store that was above plan for all five weeks.

Table P-1.   Peruvian doll sales by store

		Sales Week					
Store Number	**Store Name**	**1**	**2**	**3**	**4**	**5**	**YTD**
9841	Lovesick Lake Gift Shop	103	103	135	116	128	119
3722	Wingtip Gift & Toys	76	84	104	89	111	93
1655	Tailspin Gift & Toys	66	93	80	88	91	84
7269	Contoso, Ltd.	84	35	104	74	95	84
5460	Tkachuk Gifts	74	84	80	74	82	79

Key:

Above Plan   ■

At Plan   □

Below Plan   ■

CHAPTER 1

Understanding Business Intelligence

The story of Lisa in the Prologue, while fictitious, is actually quite relevant to the real challenges that business decision makers face everyday. From Main Street to Wall Street, the pace of business decisions continues to increase. Those companies that can create competitive advantage and craft superior business strategies in this fast-paced market will leave slow and outsmarted companies in the dust. Even though we live in the Information Age, where ever-increasing masses of data are at our disposal, we often struggle to understand what the data means. While advancements in the power of available technologies are never ending, we need to recognize that technology alone cannot solve a business problem. To drive the business forward, companies need people at the helm who can make effective decisions. Business intelligence is the key to bringing together information, people, and technology to successfully manage a company or organization. Perhaps by explaining what business intelligence has to offer a company, we can help you impact your business just as Lisa did.

Describing Business Intelligence

The term **business intelligence**, also known as **BI**, is relatively new. The term is used by different pundits and software vendors to characterize a broad range of technologies, software platforms, specific applications, and processes. Since business intelligence is a multifaceted concept, we will examine it from three different perspectives:

- Making better decisions faster
- Converting data into information
- Using a rational approach to management

Making Better Decisions Faster

The primary goal of business intelligence is to help people make decisions that improve a company's performance and promote its competitive advantage in the marketplace. In short, business intelligence empowers organizations to make *better* decisions *faster.*

In the best of all worlds, managers, from the lowest lead supervisor to the CEO, make decisions by considering their experiences, their understanding of the business, their business plan, and information. Often the experiences, understandings, and strategies that go into decision making are pretty static; that is, they change very slowly. The information, however, is always new, which means it is often changing rapidly and in a big way. It is often difficult to get a handle on these changes and understand their significance. Making *better decisions* means improving any or all parts of the process; this also results in fewer poor decisions and more superior ones. Better decisions result in better achievement of corporate objectives, such as improving shareholder value.

Business intelligence aids better decision making by analyzing whether actions are, in fact, resulting in progress toward company objectives. Deciding what is a better decision for an organization is best accomplished with a clearly stated set of objectives and a plan for achieving them. This relationship between a company's overall plan and business intelligence is not a one-way street, with business intelligence simply receiving the plan and using it as the scale for measuring the quality of decisions. Business intelligence has a major role in creating those strategies and plans. It is about making better decisions faster, and the most strategic decisions are the ones where business intelligence is the most indispensable.

What good is a well-thought-out action plan if it is simply too late to achieve competitive advantage? Most industries are highly competitive, and business opportunities are extremely time sensitive. Businesses that spot opportunities but decide too slowly how to take advantage of these opportunities will lose out to their quicker rivals. There is a need to make not only better decisions but also better decisions *faster.*

The need for speed also applies to gaining feedback within an organization. If rapid access and turnaround of information are not available, decisions are made either without information or with stale information. The negative consequences of no information or old information can be huge, such as losing a key customer or continuing to produce a product that consumers no longer prefer. While having perfect information to support every decision is an unobtainable goal, there is no doubt that making consistently better decisions sooner will provide a competitive advantage.

Converting Data into Information

To make better decisions faster, business executives and managers need relevant and useful facts at their fingertips. But there is often a large gap between the information that decision makers require and the mountains of data that businesses collect every day. We call this the **analysis gap**.

To bridge this analysis gap, organizations make significant investments in the development of BI systems to convert *raw data* into useful *information*. The most effective BI systems access huge volumes of data (measured in gigabytes and even terabytes) and deliver relevant subsets instantly to decision makers in a form to which these people can easily relate. Some call this "analysis at the speed of thought"—being able to get an answer to a question almost as quickly as the question is formulated. This makes possible a quantum leap in the quality of analysis that can be performed, which leads to a much better understanding of the business. In Chapter 2, "Bridging the Analysis Gap," we explain how BI systems support "analysis at the speed of thought."

Some people consider technology's contribution to delivering useful information as a baseline definition of business intelligence—the systems, applications, processes, and procedures that collect and convert large volumes of data into useful information for managing and controlling business activities within departments, divisions, and business units. We think this is too narrow a view.

While technology is a significant part of this process, often the hardest aspect of business intelligence is being able to define what information is useful and relevant to a decision. BI solutions at the enterprise level are charged with collecting and reporting a company's most important metrics, sometimes called **key performance indicators** (**KPIs**). KPIs guide businesses in making decisions that affect particular business units as well as the company at large. We explain more about KPIs in the section on measurement later in this chapter. In addition to KPIs, now more than ever, the vision of business intelligence has expanded beyond the internal measures that have traditionally characterized management reporting. With advancements in e-commerce, **business-to-business** (**B2B**), and

business-to-consumer (B2C) transaction systems, business intelligence is increasingly about delivering actionable information to people outside the organization—often as a revenue source.

Throughout this book, including the case studies in Part II and the practical advice in Part III, we provide details to help you understand the importance and specific techniques for converting raw data into useful decision-making information.

Using a Rational Approach to Management

Business intelligence can be described as an approach to management, an organizational state of mind, a management philosophy—in short, the *BI attitude*. People and organizations adopt the BI attitude because of a belief that a fact-based, rational approach to making decisions, to the extent this is possible, is basically a good thing.

The BI attitude is characterized as follows:

- Seeking objective measurable quantitative facts (data) about the business

- Using organized methods and technologies to analyze the facts

- Inventing and sharing models that explain the cause and effect relationships between operational actions and the effects these have on reaching the goals of the business

- Experimenting with alternate approaches and monitoring feedback on results

- Understanding that people are not always rational

- Running the business (making decisions and taking actions) based on all of these characteristics

Rationality and Science

How business intelligence applies rationality to the management of a business is reminiscent of the way science uses rationality to study the natural universe. Many aspects of science, such as collecting data, forming and testing theories, and experimenting, have parallels

---

Rationality and Science   *(continued)*

in the most rigorous BI applications. While science seeks to study isolated phenomena in meticulously controlled experimental settings, business intelligence deals with the behavior of customers, suppliers, competitors, employees, and others actors in the rough-and-tumble day-to-day conduct of business. Pure science seeks understanding for its own sake without a deadline; business intelligence seeks understanding for the purpose of taking action to meet organizational objectives.

The BI attitude of fact-based and analysis-based decision making is influencing corporate cultures everywhere, principally because we are living in a world that is becoming increasingly rich in information; the technology is available, it is getting cheaper and easier, and it is working.

Experience, gut feelings, and lightning bolts of intuition—all of these will continue as an important basis for making decisions, but more and more they are being supported by the foundation of information that business intelligence delivers. In fact, gut feelings and lightning bolts work better because they are inspired by the hard facts of business intelligence. Armed with the facts, you have excellent backup when you need to sell and promote your ideas.

Defining the BI Cycle

It is important to understand that business intelligence is even more than an attitude or an enabling technology; in fact, it is a performance management framework, an ongoing cycle by which companies set their goals, analyze their progress, gain insight, take action, measure their success, and start all over again.

Business intelligence helps managers make better decisions faster at both strategic and operating levels. Data from many sources are typically analyzed. Analysis leads to insights—many small ones, and hopefully a few big ones. These insights suggest ways to improve the business; when acted on, these insights can then be measured to see what is working. These measurements also provide more data for analysis, and the cycle starts anew. We call this progression—analysis to insight to action to measurement—the **BI cycle** (Figure 1-1).

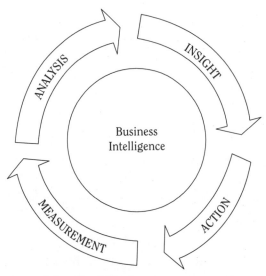

Figure 1-1.   *The BI cycle*

Analysis

When we undertake analyzing our business, how do we determine what data to collect and what analysis to perform? We do this by consciously selecting and subconsciously filtering what we think is important. This filtering is based on our basic understandings and assumptions of how our business operates, including, for example, what is important to our customers, suppliers, and employees; what factors affect product cost and quality; and what happens if we raise the selling price. This collection of everything that we think we know about how something works (in this case our business) is referred to as a **mental model**. This labeling of our understanding applies not only to people but also to organizations. Some people refer to the company's mental model as "tribal wisdom."

Vision and the Mental Model

Why are the most wildly successful companies of each generation not the ones started with the most history, money, and market share but rather those led by leaders with a vision? Is the success due to the leader or the vision? What is vision?

Vision and the Mental Model   *(continued)*

The leader has a mental model of how the world is and how the world is changing. The leader imagines a new kind of organization that is suited to take competitive advantage of these trends, and he or she sets about to create it. While a mental model explains the way the world is, a vision explains a world that may be. The leader must get many others to share the vision in order to implement a strategy to make it happen. Hugely successful organizations, the ones that establish new business paradigms, are the embodiment of radically new mental models. Business intelligence contributes significantly to this process through the BI cycle.

Mental models are essential for managers to make the many decisions that they must make at an ever-increasing pace. They are the basis on which we informally decide what we think is a good idea. Our mental models, however, can also hurt us because they can block us from seeing what might be obvious to others.

Remember Lisa? At first all she saw was the problem; it never occurred to her that she could learn something from the stores that were being successful. She assumed all stores were following her program. And the sales reporting system—a product of her company's mental model—further screened her view by delivering only fixed-format reports and assuming that reporting at the individual store level was not important for product analysis.

Having BI systems that support freestyle analysis can help you break through the limits of your current mental models and even conceptualize new ones. The abilities to drill down through layers of data, pivot rows and columns, calculate specialized metrics on the fly, and sort in any direction on any variable—all at the speed of thought—enable users to ask the questions and do the analysis in any form they choose, go down wrong paths without embarrassment or material loss of time, and work without a highly prestructured process until a clue is discovered, which then leads to a question, which then leads to an insight. Excellent analysis helps us understand our business better by allowing us to challenge conventional patterns of thinking and assumptions about what the right analysis is. Lisa didn't get an immediate answer about why the dolls were not selling, but when she started asking different questions in a more open format, a new world of possibilities opened up.

Step one of the BI cycle is to ask and answer many questions rapidly, both the conventional and the unconventional. That is what real analysis is—the freedom to be curious and ask lots of really stupid questions until you ask a brilliant one.

Insight

Insights come in different sizes. There are operational insights, such as discovering the cause of price variances in a specialized commodity purchase. There are strategic insights. For example, the best way to gain cell phone subscribers is to give away the phone and charge only for the service. On occasion, insights have created entire industries. The visionaries of computing realized that computer chips and components were becoming so small, powerful, and inexpensive that eventually everyone could own a computer; hence the personal computer was developed.

Insight is the product of broad, free-ranging analysis born of questions that only we human beings can ask—the discovery of patterns that only humans can recognize as useful. Lisa experienced several critical insights into Fabrikam's business operations because of her analysis of the data, including the realization that the gift shop on Lovesick Lake held the answer for her.

Convincing others that you have a better understanding of something is not often easy. Remember Lisa's struggle to convince her company of her great idea to expand? Her troubles were minor when compared to some historical examples of what people have gone through to shift the mental model of a large number of people. Consider the following.

Until the sixteenth century, conventional wisdom held that the earth was the center of the universe, and everything else—the sun, the moon, planets, and stars—revolved around it. This was the Ptolemaic view from which scientists developed sophisticated mathematical formulas that actually predicted celestial events such as eclipses. Then a different generation of thinkers and mathematicians had a revolutionary insight: the earth and planets revolve around the sun. This heliocentric idea was heresy, of course; it challenged political and religious foundations as well as conventional science. It was many years before it became the norm. In short, an insight per se is not always accepted just because it is brilliant or even correct.

What does this mean for business intelligence? If an individual has an important insight, it generally has to be shared by others to be useful. Just like the heliocentric model, challenges to conventional wisdom (the predominant mental model of the organization) are often unwelcome and likely to meet resistance. Well-organized business intelligence leads us to the insights, but it also provides us with the clear data, patterns, logic, reporting, graphics, calculation algorithms, and other analysis and presentation tools to help us sell the insight. Propagating insight is as much about helping people see the world in a new way and understand the benefits of this as it is about the underlying data and logic.

Action

The connection to action in the BI cycle is through the decision-making process. Action follows the better and faster decisions that business intelligence facilitates. Well-grounded and better-grounded decisions (decisions backed up by good analysis and insights) give strength and courage to the action taker. Instead of tentative decisions that often result in hedged action plans and underfunded projects, action backed by strong analysis and business intelligence is typically clearer in its purposes and details and gathers stronger organizational support for its implementation. For example, Lisa's decision to act quickly and use the dollhouse displays in other stores was not guesswork; it was a well-reasoned decision based on the analysis of data.

Finally, good business intelligence that is delivered quickly improves the cycle time for action. There is an imperative today in organizations to react more quickly, try new approaches, experiment more, and prototype faster and more frequently. BI-based decision making with faster turnaround and tighter feedback loops provides more opportunity for such action-oriented experiments and testing.

Measurement

With improved information gathering and more frequent and sometimes concurrent reporting that business intelligence brings to the table, there is greater opportunity in the organization to measure results against quantitative standards, thus leading to another cycle of analysis, insight, and corrective action.

This may sound like the old "planning and control" cycle that bean counters have made the foundation of financial management for decades. With business intelligence, however, there is a huge difference: it is not just financial management and spending controls; it is everything. Business intelligence allows the setting of standards and benchmarks for monitoring performance and providing feedback in every functional area of the business, using metrics that extend well beyond traditional financial measures.

We measure what we think is important. The BI term for the most important measures is *key performance indicators*. BI systems are specifically designed to assimilate large amounts of complex data from disparate sources and then combine the data using complicated algorithms for allocating, aggregating, and otherwise massaging the data. The result is consistent reporting on the metrics, ratios, and activity drivers—that is, the true KPIs—that managers need to understand, analyze, and take action against on a frequent basis. In a truly comprehensive BI system, no functional area of the business is untouched by its own KPIs, nor should it be. We want managers to manage what is truly manageable, and that is usually KPIs, not dollars. This is strongly facilitated by the measurement systems explicit in most BI systems.

A KPI Sampler

Here are a few examples of commonly used KPIs.

Functional Area	Typical Key Performance Indicators	
Operations	Capacity utilization	Inventory turns
	Units produced	Adherence to production plan
	# of SKUs	
	% defective	# rejects
	Direct to indirect heads	Operations headcount
	Average wait time	% orders scheduled to requested
	Yield	
	Inventory carrying cost	Returns
	Vendor performance to schedule	Inventory accuracy
		# vendors
Sales/marketing/ customer support	Unit sales	Amount sales
	Average selling price	# customers
	Amount value per customer	# products per customer
	Book-to-bill ratio	Items per order
	Sales per salesperson	Sales per employee
	# customer inquiries	
Finance	Variance vs. budget	Variance vs. forecast
	% variance	% margin
	% profit	% of sales
	Days sales outstanding	Current ratio
	Quick ratio	Asset turns
	Debt-to-equity ratio	

Enabling Business Intelligence

We have described business intelligence from several perspectives and explained the BI cycle. We are now going to explain how business intelligence can be enabled. The principal enablers are technology, people, and corporate culture.

Technology

Even the smallest company, with BI software, can do sophisticated analyses today that were unavailable to the largest organizations a generation ago. The largest companies today can create enterprise-wide BI systems that compute and monitor metrics on virtually every variable important for managing the company. How is this possible? The answer is technology—the most significant enabler of business intelligence. Let's look at the technology trends that have made modern business intelligence possible.

Processing Power

Today's desktop computers deliver more raw power than was available on supercomputers just a decade ago. The computing power of a microprocessor has reliably doubled every 18 months (Moore's law), while prices have generally held constant. The impact on business intelligence is twofold: (1) BI analysis techniques that require millions of calculations can now be done quickly on low-cost servers and distributed to client desktops at a low cost. (2) Greater processing power has revolutionized the visualization technology available—graphical views of data displayed on colorful monitors, projected on a wall for teams to share, printed, and even enhanced with real-time animation.

Data Volumes

Data storage has seen an exponential increase in capacities over the last decade, while prices have held constant or even fallen. An unprecedented amount of transaction detail is now captured, massaged, and made available for BI analysis. An analyst can load an entire copy of a business unit's sales database onto a laptop computer. The rule of thumb is the greater the quantity of data, the more certain the analysis and conclusions. As long as the BI software can load and crunch the numbers with fast turnaround, the cost of storing vast amounts of data has become insignificant compared to the benefits of better analysis.

Network Technologies

The growth of the Internet, the widespread adoption of Web browsers, and the development of user-friendly interface software have enabled organizations to connect virtually every employee to BI information databases. Business intelligence is no longer the domain of a few select department analysts who crunch numbers on their spreadsheets. Because of network technologies, it can be available to every manager and employee who needs to know what is happening in his or her own part of the business. As Bernard Liautaud[1] explains it, we are entering an era of Information Democracy.

Standards

Gone are the days when computer hardware and software had to be purchased from a single vendor. Novice users can purchase software from numerous companies, plug it into their computers, and have a high degree of confidence that the software will work. Standards enable this interoperability. BI interoperability is becoming increasingly possible primarily because of data access standards for relational and multidimensional databases that support BI systems.

BI Software

The BI software industry barely existed 10 years ago. Now several large software companies offer full suites of BI products, including tools for **extracting, transforming, and loading data (ETL)**; large-scale systems for the storage and aggregation of data; and front-end interfaces for user access—all at a fraction of the cost of the legacy, mainframe-based decision support systems that first appeared in the 1980s. The impact that the use of these tools can have on an organization's efficiency and effectiveness is enormous. In Chapter 3, "Defining BI Technologies," we describe these tools and technologies in more detail.

---

1. Author of *E-Business Intelligence: Turning Information into Knowledge into Profit* (New York: McGraw-Hill, 2000).

People

Understanding the role of people in the BI cycle allows organizations to systematically create insight and turn these insights into actions. One way in which organizations can improve their decision making is to have the right people making the decisions. This usually means a manager who is in the field and close to the customer rather than an analyst rich in data but poor in experience. In recent years "business intelligence for the masses" has been an important trend, and many organizations have made great strides in providing sophisticated yet simple analytical tools and information to a much larger user population than previously possible.

Some BI technology companies claim that their software turns data into knowledge. In our view this is marketing hype because it discounts the essential role of people. Knowledge is something people create. People are the ones who persuade others to see the world in a new way.

Today's BI technologies can analyze vast quantities of data. Inexpensive desktop computers can process more data faster than the supercomputers of a decade ago. The ability to process vast amounts of data is definitely a benefit, but suggesting that more data is the primary driver to improving business intelligence is similar to suggesting that if Sir Isaac Newton had observed more apples falling, he would have certainly developed his laws of gravity sooner. Modern managers do not suffer from a lack of data, and the technologies and techniques described later in this book provide the means to analyze that data efficiently. But no amount of raw data will substitute for experimentation and pondering. Information systems may report what is going on, but gaining insight into why this is happening requires intuiting the motivation of people and organizations. This requires people.

People are an essential element of business intelligence. But as we have observed, people can also obstruct the benefits of such intelligence because people resist changing their understandings; they like what has served them well—things with which they are comfortable. The resistance to change and the opposite of this, the eagerness to change, are often tightly woven with emotion. We saw an example of this in Lisa's story. Recall that it takes her several weeks before the data finally convinces her that the dolls are a flop. But then it takes her only a few hours to develop the conviction that she knows how to turn the situation around.

Given a set of facts, there are an infinite number of rational explanations, which are limited only by human imagination. It is not surprising then that business people, who have many motivations, will often disagree about what the data means.

Resistance to change is a problem because getting people to shift their mind-set is how organizations learn. Having models and strategies that are widely shared throughout an organization is essential for the independent decisions of numerous managers to move the organization forward, rather than working at cross purposes. Understanding our own stubbornness is useful in helping us devise strategies to persuade others. Certainly providing facts that cannot be explained by the conventional mental model, providing time for this to be grasped by all, suggesting alternative models that are consistent with the facts, and avoiding emotionally charged disputes over who is right or wrong are advisable tactics for the successful adjustment of mental models.

Let's conclude this discussion of people with an observation that may be personally relevant. BI systems serve business managers in much the way that navigation instrumentation serves a pilot; they both provide feedback information. The degree to which this instrumentation is essential depends on the size and complexity of the enterprise and the role of the manager. While a small business owner might be able to manage by dead reckoning, the head of a huge enterprise would be hopelessly overwhelmed if he or she attempted to manage without the aid of BI technologies. This observation implies that your organization's ability to grow and your success in more senior roles depend, at least in part, on having satisfactory BI technologies and a mastery of business intelligence.

Culture

A key responsibility of executives is to shape and manage corporate culture. The extent to which the BI attitude flourishes in an organization depends in large part on the organization's culture. Perhaps the most important step that an organization can take to encourage the BI attitude is the decision to measure the performance of the organization against a set of KPIs. The implied actions of publishing what the organization thinks are the most important indicators, measuring these indicators, and analyzing the results to guide improvement are nothing more than using the BI cycle.

Business intelligence can be the source of many improvements to an organization, from minor improvements in efficiency to innovative new strategies. The cultures that are most successful in enabling business intelligence are those that systematically succeed at the following:

- Providing easy and wide access to information

- Motivating wide-scale analysis and decision making

- Motivating the sharing of findings with broader audiences

- Insisting on fact-based rational support for plans

- Encouraging experimentation and tolerating "good try" failures

Finally, adopting a BI attitude is not simply something you write into a business plan, talk up at company meetings, and then expect to happen. A BI attitude has to be backed by actions. Executives cannot rationally expect better and faster decisions unless they invest in the enablers of technology and people.

Summary

Business intelligence is best understood from several perspectives: making better decisions faster, converting data into information, and using a rational approach to management. The analysis of business information leads to insights—many small ones, and hopefully a few big ones. These insights suggest ways to improve the business; when acted on, these insights are then measured to see what is working. These measurements provide more data for analysis, starting the cycle anew. We call this progression—analysis to insight to action to measurement—the BI cycle.

The enablers of the BI cycle are technology, people, and organizational culture. To achieve and maintain excellent business intelligence, these enablers require investment. Superior business intelligence is a competitive advantage that can have a huge impact on the success of an organization.

Bridging the Analysis Gap

To make better decisions faster, executives and business managers require useful information that is readily available and flexible to analyze. As you learned in Chapter 1, meeting this requirement is no trivial task—mostly because of the gap that exists between the information that business people need and the mountains of raw data that companies collect. Bridging this gap requires companies to recognize how information can be used for business analysis and to understand how computer systems convert raw data into useful information.

In this chapter, we help you understand these two concepts by (1) describing multidimensional analysis—a useful approach for viewing information that allows you to perform flexible and powerful business analysis—and (2) defining the differences between operational systems—the systems that collect a company's raw data—and BI systems—the systems that transform raw data into useful information.

Multidimensional Analysis

To help you understand what makes information useful for business analysis, let's walk through a simple, albeit extremely contrived example of BI analysis in action. Consider a fruit wholesaler who purchases fruit from farmers and transports and distributes the fruit in four markets. Let's say that you want to begin by analyzing sales—a reasonable place to start. Table 2-1 shows this information for the first and second quarters of 2001.

Table 2-1. Fruit sales for the first and second quarters of 2001

Time	Amount
Qtr 1	$16,000
Qtr 2	$16,000
Total	$32,000

According to Table 2-1, it appears that the fruit wholesaler has identical sales performance in the first and second quarters. The next step in your analysis of sales may be to examine the same sales data by a few other perspectives, for example, by the type of fruit being sold and by the market where it was sold. Table 2-2 shows this information.

Table 2-2. Three different views of fruit sales: time, market, and product

Time	Amount	Market	Amount	Product	Amount
		Atlanta	$8,000	Apples	$8,000
		Chicago	$8,000	Cherries	$8,000
Qtr 1	$16,000	Denver	$8,000	Grapes	$8,000
Qtr 2	$16,000	Detroit	$8,000	Melons	$8,000
Tot Time	$32,000	Tot Market	$32,000	Tot Product	$32,000

Note that total sales are the same—$32,000—for all three views; this is a reassuring sign. It gives you confidence that you are looking at the same information— the sales of the fruit company—but with each view broken out into different categories. Let's consider what you have just done. You have examined the overall sales broken out by three distinct categorizations—time, market, and product. These categorizations are called **dimensions**.

Based on the data presented in Table 2-2, it is not obvious what question should be asked next. At this point all you know is that sales are identical for each of the two quarters, identical for each of the four products, and identical for each of the four markets. This data is boring. There are no interesting patterns; there is little to analyze—nothing is happening. Rather than choosing a fourth dimension to categorize the sales data, let's see what happens when we combine the existing three dimensions to create a *multidimensional* view of the data (Table 2-3).

Wow! Patterns and anomalies start jumping out! Significant management information that was obscured by separate analyses of dimensions suddenly becomes obvious. For example, apples and cherries do not sell in Atlanta and Chicago in the first quarter, but grapes and melons do. It is vice versa for the second quarter. This process of interacting with multidimensional views of the data—that is, **slicing and dicing**—almost always reveals new and interesting information compared to isolated, single-dimension data lists. This is called **multidimensional analysis**. Multidimensional analysis involves viewing data simultaneously categorized along potentially many dimensions—not just three dimensions as in this example.

Table 2-3. Multidimensional view of fruit sales

		Atlanta	Chicago	Denver	Detroit	Total
Qtr 1	Apples	$ -	$ -	$2,500	$1,500	$4,000
	Cherries	$ -	$ -	$2,000	$2,000	$4,000
	Grapes	$1,000	$3,000	$ -	$ -	$4,000
	Melons	$2,000	$2,000	$ -	$ -	$4,000
	Total Q1	$3,000	$5,000	$4,500	$3,500	$16,000
Qtr 2	Apples	$4,000	$ -	$ -	$ -	$4,000
	Cherries	$1,000	$3,000	$ -	$ -	$4,000
	Grapes	$ -	$ -	$1,500	$2,500	$4,000
	Melons	$ -	$ -	$2,000	$2,000	$4,000
	Total Q2	$5,000	$3,000	$3,500	$4,500	$16,000
	Grand Total	$8,000	$8,000	$8,000	$8,000	$32,000

Operational Systems

You might think that multidimensional analysis is an obvious way to analyze data, and you are right; multidimensional analysis is very intuitive for businesspeople because it represents a natural, easy, and effective way to analyze information. The more difficult task is getting data into a format that supports multidimensional analysis at the speed of thought.

To help you understand what we mean, let's first consider where a company's data originates. The sales information from the fruit wholesaler originated with each customer placing an order for specific fruit products. Each customer order was then stored in a database that was especially designed to track the order throughout its entire lifecycle. We call this type of database an **operational database** because its job is to support the day-to-day operations of the company. Even though data is captured and stored in an operational database, the data is not necessarily readily available for business analysis. The opposite is usually true. These databases are structured for the purposes of running the day-to-day business by processing *transactions*. They are not structured for effective business analysis.

OLTP Systems

While their underlying technologies have changed dramatically over time, operational databases still have the same basic functionality: to gather, update, store, retrieve, and archive data. In simplest terms, a rotary card file of addresses is a database. At the high end, a large enterprise stores and manages billions of records, taking up terabytes of storage in a database structure called a **relational database management system** or **RDBMS**.[1] Collectively, operational systems are frequently called **online transaction processing (OLTP)** systems.

To help you understand how an OLTP system works, let's walk through a common OLTP example—withdrawing cash from an automatic teller machine (ATM). You walk up to the ATM and slip in your card; it reads your account profile. You punch in your secret code; it verifies the code. You punch in an amount to withdraw; it dishes up the money and delivers a receipt showing your adjusted balance. You are interacting with an OLTP system, and this activity has three characteristics that fundamentally define the system:

- It processes a *transaction:* you are withdrawing cash according to the rules of the game, which are correct account, correct password, money in account, and so forth. This is the rock bottom or lowest level of business activity for a bank.

- It performs all the elements of the transaction in *real time:* verifies who you are, gives you the money, immediately updates your account, and so forth. Everything about the transaction occurs more or less simultaneously.

---

1. The language for accessing data (also called querying) in an RDBMS is an industry standard called **SQL** (pronounced *sequel*), which stands for **structured query language**.

- It processes many transactions on a *continuous basis:* your account
  and the accounts of others making deposits, withdrawals, and other
  account-based transactions are processed continuously—all day,
  every day. There are no rigid cutoffs, stops, or starts—at least none
  apparent to customers stepping up to the ATM.

OLTP systems are everywhere: order tracking, invoicing, credit card processing, retail bar code scanning, inventory control, personnel management,
banking, travel reservations, telephone call processing, online browsing, and
more. OLTP is designed for managing the raw data of business, which
requires efficiency and up-to-the-minute processing of transactions at the
lowest level of detail.

So why not use these same OLTP systems for business analysis? The
answer lies in the questions you want efficiently answered. For example, "Did
John Doe withdraw cash today, and if so, how much?" is a transaction question quickly answered by the OLTP system without much fuss. While this
data can be served up quickly, it is not very useful for an analysis of the overall business.

"As a trend over the past six months, what has been the average number
of transactions per ATM station per day in Cucamonga, California, outside
regular banking hours? Which are the busiest ATMs? Which ATMs are seeing
the fastest growth in usage?" These are potentially interesting questions that
might affect the number and location of ATMs, but they are not questions
you would ask of an OLTP system. There are too many records to search,
sort, and summarize; mathematical calculations are also required to obtain
the answer (averaging for all machines). Imposing these types of queries on
the OLTP system on a regular basis would likely interfere with the main
business of getting banking done.

While OLTP systems are lousy for analysis, they do, however, gather the
raw data that is the foundation for type of multidimensional analysis that we
saw for the fruit wholesaler. And that is the challenge businesses face. It is
those millions of transactions in operational systems (typically multiple
OLTP systems in larger organizations) that are the rich basis of data that
needs to be converted into useful information for business analysis. Getting
it there is not simple—especially when the data resides within multiple, dis-
parately organized, and often old technology systems.

Operational Reporting

Historically, IT departments spend the majority of their resources programming and maintaining operational systems. In today's environment, however, such systems are almost always purchased as packaged software applications. These applications typically include meaningful reporting capabilities, which have value for performing business analysis and are rightly part of an overall BI strategy. Unfortunately virtually all suffer from the following two basic limitations.

The first limitation is that they report on only their own internally gathered information without the ability to combine data or absorb structures from other systems. This situation, where reporting from one system is essentially blind to the data from other systems, is described as "stovepipe reporting" or "silos of data." When you report from these silos, it is difficult to create a broad set of metrics and key performance indicators (KPIs) that combine data from multiple systems. For example, revenues per employee (a typical productivity measure in many industries) is computed by combining revenue data from the order management system and employee data from the human resources system.

The second basic limitation of operational reporting is that it typically does not effectively support multidimensional analysis at the speed of thought. It is significantly slower, less intuitive, and less flexible than required.

Business Intelligence Systems

For these and other reasons, some type of **BI system**—a place where data from many operational systems (and possibly outside data sources) is pulled together for the purpose of analysis—is an inevitable part of every large organization's infrastructure. Fortunately, all operational systems have export capabilities, and operational application vendors, understanding the limitation of stovepipe reporting, are increasingly designing their systems to be more easily integrated with "downstream" BI systems. Chapter 3 presents the common components of BI systems.

In this chapter, we focus on the components of the BI system that enable delivery of fast and efficient multidimensional analysis. When multidimensional analysis is supported by interface tools and database structures that allow instantaneous access and easy user manipulation, a specific BI paradigm comes to life: **online analytical processing**.

Why Online Analytical Processing?

Online analytical processing (OLAP) got its name because this name contrasts well with online transaction processing (OLTP), a term that was already in widespread use when the term *OLAP* was created. E. F. Codd, who coined the term *OLAP* (and one of the original gurus of relational database technology), evidently wanted to highlight the fundamental differences between transaction processing and analytical processing. In 1993 he articulated a broad set of criteria for OLAP databases. Subsequently, many vendors have jumped on the OLAP bandwagon, delivering systems with an extremely wide range of features and functionality but not all rigidly applying Codd's criteria. Practically speaking, the "why OLAP?" question for business intelligence can be answered by considering three critically important capabilities that all OLAP systems must incorporate with a high level of efficiency.

OLAP first provides a conceptual and intuitive data model that users who are not necessarily trained as analysts can understand and quickly relate to. This model is actually called multidimensional analysis—being able to see data through multiple filters, or dimensions as we call them, all at once. As we stated earlier, the best managers and analysts were already multidimensional thinkers—even before OLAP—asking questions such as the following:

- "What are actual sales compared to forecast sales by region by salesperson by product?"
- "What is our profitability by product and by customer?"
- "What is our backlog by product by customer and by time?"

Region, salesperson, customer, product, and time (the *by*, *by*, *by* things) are typical dimensions for business activities. Sales, profitability, and backlog are called **measures**. Unlike standard relational databases, where dimensionality is in the data but obscure, OLAP systems organize the data directly as multidimensional structures, including easy-to-use tools for users to get at the information in multiple and simultaneous dimensional views. More on this subject will be covered later in this chapter.

OLAP is also fast for the user. It is the quick response for getting information back from the OLAP system that allows the "speed of thought" experience we mentioned in Chapter 1. Fast retrieval times let managers and analysts ask and answer more questions in a concentrated period of time than ever before, thus addressing the "infinite question" syndrome, where every interesting pattern and useful piece of information in a database can be theoretically explored.

Finally OLAP systems have robust calculation engines for handling the specialized calculation requirements that a multidimensional structure imposes. Think about having to write spreadsheet formulas that interlink as many as ten dimensions, such as time, region, product, customer, channel, organization structure, and so forth. (This process is not easy for most human beings.) OLAP calculation engines structure the data in a way that allows the business analyst to write simple, straightforward formulas that perform *across* multiple dimensions with only a few lines of code.

OLAP System Structures

The power of OLAP comes from structuring the data in a manner aligned with the way that people naturally perform analysis. In this section we walk through each of the fundamental OLAP concepts—dimensions, hierarchies, and measures.

Dimensions for Slice and Dice

Simply defined, a dimension is a categorically consistent view of data—that is, all the members within a dimension, such as products, belong together as a group. There are two simple tests for this:

- Data about the members can be compared; for example, the actual and forecast members of a scenario dimension can be compared.

- Data from the members can be aggregated to summary members; for example, the members January, February, and March of a time dimension can be aggregated to a value for Quarter 1.

As you saw in the example at the beginning of the chapter, an interesting notion about dimensions is the ability to *slice and dice* multidimensional data as, for example, we might slice and then dice a tomato. To understand this, think of the slice as being a specific member of a dimension, for example, product A in the product dimension. When we dice in OLAP, we are creating a series of intersections for a given slice with data from other dimensions. We can view sales for product A, for example, *by* month, *by* region, and *by* customer. *By* indicates how we are dicing the data. It is this multidimensional intersection of data and how it is organized in an OLAP database that make multidimensional analysis especially interesting—and powerful. The ability to intuitively and instantaneously switch views is a basic feature of all respectable OLAP user tools.

Another capability inherent in OLAP's multidimensional design is the **pivoting** and nesting of dimensions, which are both point-and-click manipulations incorporated in sound OLAP systems (Table 2-4).

Table 2-4 shows the same data as in Table 2-3, but this time the products have been pivoted from a row orientation to a column orientation (that is, apples, cherries, grapes, and melons are now across the top), and markets were pivoted from columns to rows (that is, Atlanta, Chicago, Denver, and Detroit are now rows). In addition, the quarters have been flipped on the row axis to an inside nested row position. We can now see the column totals for products that were not summarized in Table 2-3.

In summary, OLAP systems organize data by multidimensional intersections. This organization, accompanied by interface tools for pivoting and nesting dimensions, allows users to rapidly view detailed values, patterns, variances, and anomalies in the data that are otherwise obscured by single dimensional analysis. The greater the number of dimensions (within reasonable limits), the greater the depth of analysis.

Table 2-4. Pivoting and nesting data

		Apples	Cherries	Grapes	Melons	Total
Atlanta	Qtr 1	$ -	$ -	$1,000	$2,000	$3,000
	Qtr 2	$4,000	$1,000	$ -	$ -	$5,000
	Total Qtrs	$4,000	$1,000	$1,000	$2,000	$8,000
Chicago	Qtr 1	$ -	$ -	$3,000	$2,000	$5,000
	Qtr 2	$ -	$3,000	$ -	$ -	$3,000
	Total Qtrs	$ -	$3,000	$3,000	$2,000	$8,000
Denver	Qtr 1	$2,500	$2,000	$ -	$ -	$4,500
	Qtr 2	$ -	$ -	$1,500	$2,000	$3,500
	Total Qtrs	$2,500	$2,000	$1,500	$2,000	$8,000
Detroit	Qtr 1	$1,500	$2,000	$ -	$ -	$3,500
	Qtr 2	$ -	$ -	$2,500	$2,000	$4,500
	Total Qtrs	$1,500	$2,000	$2,500	$2,000	$8,000
	Grand Total	$8,000	$8,000	$8,000	$8,000	$32,000

Analysis capabilities aside, multidimensional data in an OLAP system is typically visualized as a **cube** storage structure with lots of "mini-cubes," or *cells* as they are more commonly called, making up the cube as a whole. Figure 2-1 is a picture of the cube that would house the simplified data for the fruit seller.

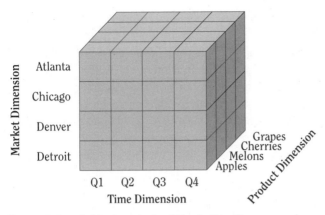

Figure 2-1. *Cubical analysis of the fruit-selling example*

Each cell contains a value, which is the value of sales for the intersection of each unique combination of market, time period, and product. For example, the value of the cell for apples for Atlanta in the second quarter is $4,000. The value of all cells as we saw from Tables 2-1 to 2-4 is $32,000.

Let's look at the cube again, this time highlighting a slice as it might be depicted on an OLAP-generated report (Figure 2-2).

The cherries member of the product dimension crosses over all intersections of the time and market dimensions. The sum of these highlighted cells is the total sales for cherries, which is $8,000. Again, slicing and dicing in the OLAP world is calling up subsets of cells that the user has selected to view from the master OLAP cube stored on a data server.

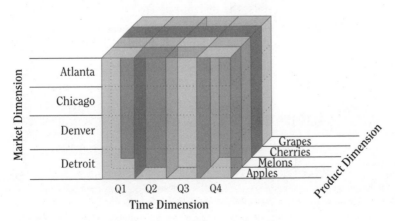

Figure 2-2. *Multidimensional analysis of fruit selling*

In the real world, however, an OLAP cube may commonly have dozens of dimensions with hundreds, thousands, or even millions of members in a given dimension. Therefore, calling an OLAP database a cube is a metaphor, not an actual storage structure. The true definition of an OLAP cube is an n-dimensional structure that stores and maintains discrete intersection values. Some OLAP database architectures may also include multiple cubes with intersections between them.

Hierarchies for Drill Down

Assume you are a product manager for Fabrikam Corporation (remember Lisa's company from the Prologue?). Your task is to perform a thorough analysis of units, average prices, and amount sales for 100 specific products that Fabrikam sells. Your analysis includes looking at patterns across 24 months for 100 customers in 20 districts in Canada.

How many data points might you have to consider? The answer is 14,400,000, which is computed by multiplying 3 measures (units, average price, and amount sales) by 100 products by 24 months by 100 customers by 20 districts. Of course, not all customers are represented in all districts, and not all customers buy all products, but can you really know who buys what and where? The multidimensional analysis is not made any easier by the fact that not all customers buy in all regions.

This analysis problem is addressed in OLAP systems that allow you to organize the data into hierarchies that aggregate the detail to higher and higher levels. For example, the monthly data can be *rolled up* (that is, summarized) to quarter and year totals, the districts rolled up to regions, the products rolled up to product lines and product groups, and so forth. Average prices can also be back calculated (that is, amount divided by units) at each level in the hierarchy from the aggregations of the units and amount sales.

The multidimensional analysis we explored in the previous section becomes manageable because the hierarchical organization of each dimension allows you to start at the top of the hierarchy and *drill down*[2] through

---

2. The use of the word *drill* in OLAP systems has a very specific meaning. *Drill down* is the action of clicking a member name to see the next lower level of detail in the hierarchy. *Drill up* is clicking a member to see the next highest level (that is, a bottom-up action). *Drill across* opens up a new dimension. *Drill through* is clicking a summarized data value to display the source data rows that comprise that value.

the data as you see interesting patterns or anomalies. This *top-down* approach of analysis is similar to the game of 20 questions. You start by asking broad questions; then depending on the answers, you ask increasingly focused questions; finally you figure out the correct answer. Young children are not very good at this game, but adults are. Thinking top-down is a natural way for people to organize complex information, but it is also a learned behavior that takes some practice.

Multidimensional data organized into **hierarchies** is an intuitively comfortable way for analyzing the mountains of data available from OLTP systems. The mechanics of OLAP interfaces—especially pointing and clicking to *drill down* into interesting layers—is made possible by the lightning speed with which queries are answered. This functionality gives managers and analysts a completely new process for dealing with large amounts of data, a process called **ad hoc analysis**.

Paper-based reporting with fixed formats presumes a set list of questions that requires answers. Ad hoc analysis has no such constraints:

- Virtually any question (in a well-constructed OLAP system) can be answered in real time with a few minutes of drill down.

- Virtually any report can be formatted (or graphed) with pivoting and nesting of dimensions.

- Virtually anyone in the company, including executives who like to ask lots of questions, can be taught how to do it with minimal training.

The design of OLAP cubes—deciding what dimensions to include, what level of detail to pull from OLTP systems, how to define the hierarchies, and other elements—is important to the user's experience and the usefulness of the system for ad hoc analysis. (In Chapters 9 and 10 we provide some practical advice for making these choices.) The user needs to understand the terminology of dimensions and especially hierarchies, which is common in most OLAP systems, in order to perform ad hoc analysis. To help you understand the vocabulary of dimensions, we are going to use common OLAP terms to describe the dimension pictured in Figure 2-3:

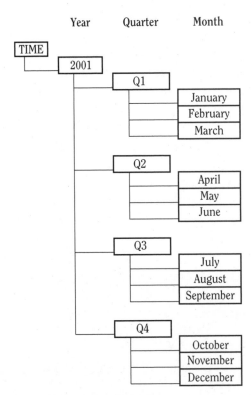

Figure 2-3. *Time dimension*

- **Dimension:** A categorically consistent group of members represented as a specific axis of an OLAP cube. Figure 2-3 is a representation of a time dimension. In addition to time, common dimensions for business analysis include customers, products, geographic regions, distribution channels, employee categories, and so forth. Typical OLAP cubes have seven or eight dimensions, although dozens are possible.

- **Hierarchy:** The organization of *levels* within a dimension that reflects (1) how additive data is aggregated level by level and (2) the top-down drill down path for users within the dimension. In Figure 2-3 the hierarchy is a general calendar organization of the levels: year, quarter, and month. A **ragged hierarchy** is one where drill down levels are not parallel, for example, when path A is five levels deep from the top level to the lowest level, but path B is only 3 levels deep. An **alternate hierarchy** is a second organization of aggregation levels that uses the same bottom-level data for roll-up as the main hierarchy does; for example, the statutory chart of accounts roll-up would be an alternate hierarchy to the management chart of accounts roll-up. Both use the same source of bottom-level data.

- **Member:** The name or label for any member at any level in a hierarchy. Bottom-level members are sometimes called **leaf members**. In Figure 2-3, 2001, Q1, January, February, and March are all members; January, February, and March are the leaf members.

- **Family Relationships:** Terminology used for describing the relationships between members within a hierarchy. The most commonly used family names are as follows:

  - *Child:* A member directly subordinate to another member in a hierarchy. For example, January is a child of the Q1.

  - *Parent:* A member directly above another member in a hierarchy. For example, Q1 is a parent of January.

  - *Sibling:* A member at the same level as one or more other members sharing the same parent. For example, January, February, and March are siblings of each other.

  - *Descendant:* Any member at any lower level in relation to another specific member. For example, all quarters and months for 2001 are descendants of the member 2001.

  - *Ancestor:* Any member at any higher level in relation to another member. For example, the members Q1 and 2001 are ancestors of January.

To supplement your analysis, you will most likely also have descriptive information that is not a part of a hierarchy but still important to your analysis. This nonhierarchical information is known as attributes or member properties. Examples of attributes include employee hire date, model, size, list price, and color.

What Are You Measuring?

We have described how you can structure and view data in an OLAP database using dimensions and hierarchies. Yet we have not focused on what you are measuring: "What is the nature of the data being aggregated, stored, calculated, and otherwise analyzed?"

The data in most BI applications and all OLAP systems is called a measure. In its simplest definition, a measure is any quantitative expression. For example, amount sales is an important measure for analyzing sales activity (as we saw in the examples earlier in this chapter by the fictitious fruit seller). In OLAP (and this is an important qualification), a measure is what is being analyzed *across multiple dimensions,* for example, unit sales *by* month, *by* product, and *by* customer. (The words *across* and *by* have the same OLAP meaning.) The measure is unit sales, and each intersection of the three dimensions has a different unit sales value. The total of unit sales is the sum of the values of all combinations of members at the lowest level.

The following are four important parameters for what measures are and how they work in OLAP:

- A measure is *always a quantity* or an expression that yields a quantity.

- A measure can take *any quantitative format,* for example, an absolute value (unit sales), a currency value (amount sales), a percentage (percent sales), or a ratio (sales per head).

- A measure can be derived from *any original data source or calculation,* for example, a direct input (unit sale for a transaction), an aggregation (sum of unit sales), an average (an average of selling price), a formula (amount sales divided by heads), a count (number of customers), and so forth.

- You must have at least *one measure* to do any type of OLAP analysis; an application will typically have many different measures and in some extreme cases thousands of measures.

The measures being analyzed depend on the purpose of the OLAP system. For example, unit sales and sales per salesperson are important measures for the sales department. Inventory turns and debt-to-equity ratio are standard calculations in balance sheet analysis. Same store sales are a fundamental measure for large retail operations. Burn rate is an important cash management metric for venture-financed start-ups.

Measures in business intelligence are generally known by different names, depending on the application. For example, the terms *metric* and *key performance indicator* are used interchangeably to represent important measures that you should pay attention to. The term **benchmark** refers to a measure used for making comparisons, for example, industry-specific ratios such as a price/earnings ratio. A **ratio** is a measure where the result is calculated specifically from dividing one measure by another, such as sales per salesperson.

As previously mentioned, a special feature of OLAP is the ability to write simple formulas that automatically calculate across multiple dimensions. This conceptual approach to calculation allows OLAP analysts and administrators to perform extremely complicated calculations typically not possible in a normal spreadsheet environment. For example, the grail for finance and marketing has been to calculate customer profitability—the customer dimension parallel for product line profitability. The difficulty for spreadsheets has been cross-dimensional challenges—that is, product, marketing, and customer support costs residing in different OLTP systems and associated with different dimensions. With integration of multiple OLTP data into data warehouses and the multidimensional calculation engine of OLAP, reasonably accurate customer profitability analysis is now possible, though it is still not easy.

OLAP Storage Modes

OLAP systems support multidimensional analysis at the speed of thought by storing data in structures that are optimized to provide fast data retrieval. Behind the scenes, OLAP systems can store data in different locations depending on what your analysis needs are and what options a particular OLAP vendor offers. The general businessperson is probably not going to be too concerned with how an OLAP system stores data to meets his or her analysis needs. However, those who are going to participate in the selection of OLAP systems for your company—something that we recommend businesspeople be involved in—need to be familiar with the terms that describe how OLAP systems store data. (In Chapter 10 we provide practical advice on how businesspeople can participate in technology decisions, such as the selection of an OLAP system.)

Most OLAP systems typically utilize one or many of the following three storage paradigms to support multidimensional analysis: desktop files, relational database servers, and multidimensional database servers. Let's take a closer look at each of these.

- Desktop files (known as **desktop online analytical processing [DOLAP]**). Because data is stored on individual desktop machines, you will tend to find DOLAP existing by itself in smaller-scale applications where there is minimal need for multiple users to have access to a single data source on a central server. You will also find DOLAP as a part of many OLAP vendors' overall offering to facilitate analysis when users are away from their company network, such as when they are on an airplane.

- Relational databases servers (known as **relational online analytical processing [ROLAP]**). You will find lots of ROLAP environments in various size implementations. Storing data in a relational database allows you to take advantage of one of its greatest benefits—being able to store lots of data. What tends to happen, however, is that the data retrieval performance for ROLAP will often not be as fast as other storage options, such as multidimensional servers. Some OLAP vendors store data only in relational databases regardless of the data volume. Other vendors provide ROLAP as one of several options.

- Multidimensional databases servers (known as **multidimensional online analytical processing [MOLAP]**). In MOLAP storage, data is placed into special structures that are stored on a central server(s). MOLAP tends to offer the greatest data retrieval performance— generally outperforming all other storage modes. However, there are some arguments that MOLAP cannot handle as much data as ROLAP. The performance and storage really depend on the particular OLAP product and the type of analysis that you are trying to accomplish.

For the sake of thoroughness, we would be remiss if we did not mention the fourth storage mode: **HOLAP (hybrid online analytical processing)**. HOLAP is not really a distinct mode of storing data. Rather, HOLAP is the ability to spread data across both relational and multidimensional databases in order to get the best of both worlds. Whether this is true or not depends on the particular vendor.

For business users the storage mode is transparent—or at least it should be. Businesspeople don't care whether an OLAP system uses MOLAP, ROLAP, DOLAP, or HOLAP. What business users will pay attention to is how much effort they need to expend and how long they have to wait in order to perform fast and flexible analysis of their data. With this in mind, OLAP systems need to use whatever storage mode is appropriate to give users the best possible experience.

Summary

The gap between raw data and business information can be bridged through a series of processes that start with OLTP systems (where the data is collected) and end with BI systems (where the data is organized into dimensions, hierarchies, and measures for analysis). OLAP systems enable ad hoc analysis and on-the-fly construction of specialized reports by allowing users to slice and dice their data by different dimensions, pivoting rows and columns, and drilling down through hierarchies. These standard OLAP system capabilities allow users to quickly ask and answer questions and identify patterns and anomalies otherwise obscured by single-dimensional analysis.

Designing effective multidimensional systems lies within the specific construction of the dimensions, hierarchies, and measures. Understanding the terminology and mechanics of each are essential to building BI systems that truly meet the end user's needs and deliver the "speed of thought" experience.

Defining BI Technologies

In Chapter 2 we described how BI platforms enable organizations to bridge the analysis gap between the data that their operational systems collect and the information that business decision makers require. When a company decides to implement a BI platform, there are choices that need to be made regarding the type of platform that will be constructed and the specific tools and technologies that will be used to convert raw data into useful information. While decisions such as these typically fall into the realm of information technology (IT) professionals, businesspeople need to actively participate in these decisions to make sure that a company's BI platform adequately supports its analysis needs.

To help you participate in this process, this chapter serves as an easy-to-use guide for understanding BI technologies. The technical terms that we define and use in this chapter will not only supply you with the knowledge to effectively communicate with IT professionals when you need to make BI platform decisions but also help you understand and appreciate the technical details of the BI case studies in Part II. In addition, learning this terminology will help you derive the most benefit from Chapter 10, "Implementing a BI Solution," where we provide practical advice for making BI technology decisions.

The High-Level View

The process that BI platforms use to capture raw data and convert it into useful information may be simple or very complicated. A common BI platform that many organizations use to support their BI initiatives is the data warehouse system. The data warehouse system contains several components that work together to supply data to business decision makers. To help you understand what these components are and how they work together, we first take a high-level view, answering two basic questions about the flow of data in the data warehouse system: (1) Where is data stored? and (2) How does data get to business users?

Where Data Is Stored

As explained in Chapter 2, data comes from the operational systems that support the day-to-day transactions of the business. A company or business unit of a large corporation may have dozens of operational systems. These systems can be line-of-business applications such as human resource systems and supply chain systems, enterprise resource planning (ERP) applications, or customer resource management (CRM) systems. These operational systems are extremely efficient at supporting transactional processes; however, they are not very effective at supporting business analysis, especially when the analysis requires compiling data from multiple data sources.

Knowing the limitations of operational systems, many companies meet their business reporting and analysis needs by gathering data from their operational systems and storing that data in a collective repository. This repository not only has a special name that you may already be familiar with—the **data warehouse**—but it also identifies where data is stored in this BI platform.

When we say that a data warehouse is a collective repository of data, we do not necessarily mean that it is a single data store. Many experts define the data warehouse as a centralized store that feeds into a series of subject-specific stores, called **data marts**, as depicted in Figure 3-1.

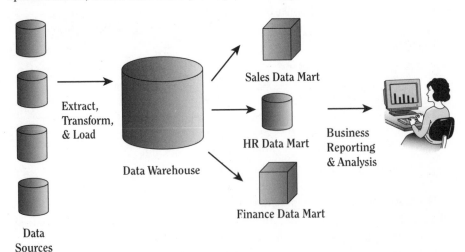

Figure 3-1. *The enterprise data warehouse*

Others accept a broader definition of the data warehouse to be a collection of data marts, as depicted in Figure 3-2.

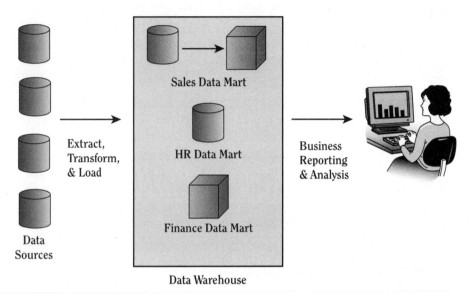

Figure 3-2.   *The collection of data*

The common denominator in both definitions is the concept of a subject-specific data mart. While data marts are "subject-specific," what constitutes a subject varies from organization to organization depending on the type of analysis that needs to be performed. For example, a company may build a data mart to support the sales department's need to analyze product sales performance and profit margins. The same company may have another data mart that allows the human resources department to analyze trends in headcount and average number of work days for each employee.

Whatever data warehouse definition you adopt, it is important to understand that the data warehouse should not consist of independent silos of data. If it contained independent silos, analyzing such data would be no better than reporting directly from the operational systems! Rather, in a data warehouse, common dimensions and measures can be easily shared. This sharing is important not only to make sure that dimensions and measures have common meanings across a company but also to support the calculation of metrics that combine data from different operational systems.

For example, in Chapter 2, you saw that a metric such as revenue per employee is difficult to directly calculate from operational systems because you need data from the order management system silo and data from the human resources system silo. In the data warehouse, however, this metric can be easily calculated by combining sales data from the sales data mart and employee data from the human resources data mart based on shared dimensions such as time and employee. The more data that can be shared across business processes, the more powerful your business analysis will be.

As you might guess, integrating data can involve a great deal of work especially when you have mountains of data that come from multiple operational systems. There is a special set of processes, collectively known as **ETL** processes, whose purpose is to extract, transform, and load data from one or many operational systems into the data warehouse. Although businesspeople typically do not have much direct exposure to the details of the ETL processes, they do participate in defining the business rules that drive how data is integrated. The business rules are usually determined based on the type of analysis that is to be performed and how well the data supports those analysis requirements.

How Data Gets to Business Users

Once loaded into the data warehouse, **business reporting and analysis processes** are responsible for taking data from the data warehouse, assembling it into a business-friendly format (such as spreadsheets, charts, and graphs), and delivering this information to business users. To implement this process, there is a category of software, loosely called **front-end tools**, that harvests the information from the data warehouse and present this information to users in the form of reports and interactive views. Data can also be investigated using more advanced analysis technology such as **data mining** to find data patterns that explain behavior or uncover trends that are hard to see with the naked eye. While the specifics of these processes will depend on the needs of the business users, the overriding goal of these processes is to put useful data into the hands of business decision makers to help them make better decisions faster.

Now that you have a high-level view of how data flows from operational systems to business users, the rest of this chapter focuses on describing in detail the most significant components of the data warehouse architecture. However, instead of following the flow of data from source system to business user, we start with the component that businesspeople care about the most—the reporting and analysis processes.

Reporting and Analysis

Of all the components of the data warehouse architecture, reporting and analysis is probably the one that business users are most familiar with because its primary purpose is to put data into their hands. To make this experience beneficial for business users, reporting and analysis processes need to assemble data into a format that is meaningful to different types of businesspeople.

Making Data Easy to Analyze

As you learned in Chapter 2, making data understandable and useful for business users is one of the primary motivations behind multidimensional analysis. We quickly saw how easy it was to spot interesting trends in the fruit wholesaler's data when we examined a table that displayed sales data along the time, market, and product dimensions. Although tabular grids are a great way of consolidating data, it is also important for business users to see data displayed graphically using charts and other visualization techniques. Often these graphics work hand-in-hand with tables to provide users with different perspectives on the data.

For a sense of the power that such graphics provide, let's look at a classic yet fictitious example[1] that we have modified slightly for clarity. Let's say you have 4 departments, each with 11 employees, and you want to analyze whether tenure with the company has any relation to the number of days that people are absent each year. The data for the 4 departments is presented in Table 3-1.

Table 3-1.   Tenure and sick days by department

Department One		Department Two	
Tenure	Sick Days	Tenure	Sick Days
10.0	8.04	10.0	9.14
8.0	6.95	8.0	8.14
13.0	7.58	13.0	8.74
9.0	8.81	9.0	8.77
11.0	8.33	11.0	9.26
14.0	9.96	14.0	8.1
6.0	7.24	6.0	6.13

1. F. J. Anscombe, Graphs in Statistical Analysis, *American Statistician,* 27 (February 1973), 17–21.

Table 3-1. Tenure and sick days by department *(continued)*

Department One		Department Two	
Tenure	**Sick Days**	**Tenure**	**Sick Days**
4.0	4.26	4.0	3.1
12.0	10.84	12.0	9.13
7.0	4.82	7.0	7.26
5.0	5.68	5.0	4.74
Department Three		**Department Four**	
Tenure	**Sick Days**	**Tenure**	**Sick Days**
10.0	7.46	8.0	6.58
8.0	6.77	8.0	5.76
13.0	12.74	8.0	7.71
9.0	7.11	8.0	8.84
11.0	7.81	8.0	8.47
14.0	8.84	8.0	7.04
6.0	6.08	8.0	5.25
4.0	5.39	19.0	12.5
12.0	8.15	8.0	5.56
7.0	6.42	8.0	7.91
5.0	5.763	8.0	6.89

The average tenure for each department is 9.0, and the average number of sick days is 7.5 for each. Most people could study these four tables for hours and not gain much insight. But most people who examine the graphical representations of the same data in Figure 3-3 see very obvious differences and patterns, not nearly so obvious in the tables.

When presented in an appropriate graphical format, information and insight practically jump off the page. This makes the case quite clearly: the strategy for business reporting and analysis must consider the best method of presenting data to business users—whether it is tables, charts, or graphs.

Defining User Communities

Up to now we have been referring to business users as one generic group of people. From a reporting and analysis perspective, business users usually fall into one of three distinct users communities depending on their specific

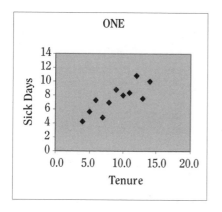

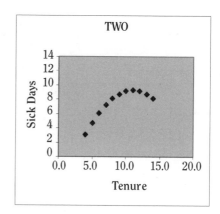

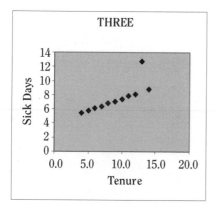

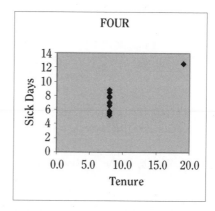

Figure 3-3. *Tenure and sick days by department*

analysis needs: the information user, the information consumer, and the power analyst. While all these user communities may not apply in every situation, it is important to understand how each group typically reports and analyzes information. Sometimes it is helpful to picture these users in a pyramid (see Figure 3-4).

The Information User

At the bottom of the user pyramid are information users, often the largest part of a business community. The information user generally requires standard reports, which may be brief or extended, and that often include charts as well as tables. The information user wants to scan consistently structured reports without needing slice or dice to find the desired values. This typically

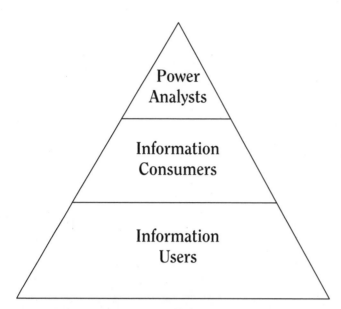

Figure 3-4. *Business user communities*

involves creating static or simple interactive reports, either in printed form or as static HTML pages or other documents.

The Information Consumer

The information consumer requires the ability to dynamically query the database, without becoming an expert at database design or the query tool. The information consumer typically wants a "guided" user experience that allows pivoting and nesting when desired, while eliminating options that may create undesirable results. With an interactive solution at hand that provides ad hoc multidimensional analysis, many businesspeople cross the line between information users and information consumers.

The Power Analyst

At the top of the pyramid are the power analysts who require the full analytical power of the data mart in order to perform free-form ad hoc analysis. The power analyst is willing to learn the details of database design and the query tool in order to obtain the necessary results. The power analyst often creates reports that will be used by others. Of the three groups, this one has the fewest members.

Using Front-End Tools

To implement the reporting and analysis process, front-end tools harvest data from the data warehouse and present it to business users in the form of reports and interactive views. The front-end tools that support business reporting and analysis can be roughly grouped into two primary categories:

- *Tools that follow a reporting paradigm:* These tools tend to excel at producing tabular reports. Many of these tools are now fairly mature in providing Web browser interfaces for designing and viewing reports suitable for very wide-scale deployments. They also frequently have very strong printing and scheduling capabilities.

- *Tools that follow the multidimensional ad hoc data exploration paradigm:* These tools tend to excel at reading OLAP cubes, supporting interactive analysis, and providing graphical views.

As you would expect, there is much competition among front-end tool vendors, each offering a wide range of functionality and features for making the standard reporting and ad hoc analysis fast and easy to use. Features, however, are not the same as benefits. Product features that address capabilities for ad hoc analysis may provide considerable benefit for power analysts who spend a lot of time exploring the data but may not be important for information users who need strong report formatting and distribution capabilities. Thus, when designing BI systems, companies must invest time in understanding the broader BI objectives and specific needs of their users and sort out vendor choices based on these objectives and needs. This topic will be explored in more detail in Chapter 10. The good news is that there are a lot of choices, and the user interface technologies for business intelligence continue to expand rapidly.

Applying Data Mining

While the top-down analysis supported by front-end tools is the most common approach for business intelligence used today, data mining is a bottom-up approach that is becoming increasingly popular as another means of analyzing data to make better informed decisions. Instead of using summary data as a starting point for analyzing trends, data mining can be used to analyze relationships in detailed data, which can then answer questions related to which customers should be targeted for a new product or which customers are most likely to take their business elsewhere.

Data mining is a term that comes from the metaphor of using a computer to sift through mountains of data, searching for gems of information similar to mining for real, precious stones. The gems of information are meaningful and unexpected patterns or clusters of data. While these patterns can simply be statistical anomalies that do not indicate any cause-and-effect relationship, sometimes they lead to valuable insights.

Once limited to the academic domain, where knowledge is considered to have value regardless of its application, data mining is gaining acceptance in the business world. Pharmaceutical companies have saved millions of dollars by using sophisticated data mining techniques to determine which chemical combinations are most likely to produce useful drugs. Companies that use database marketing extensively have dramatically reduced costs, without a reduction in revenue, by using data mining to send mailings only to those customers who are most likely to respond. Similarly, companies whose revenue is closely tied to long-term relationships with customers have used data mining to identify profitable customers who are most likely to be lured away by the competition. Special incentives are then offered to these customers to encourage them to stay or to use other services that may more closely fit their needs. In all these cases, data mining proved valuable because the cost of acquiring these insights was far less than the impact on corporate profits as a result of lowered costs or increased revenue.

If data mining is so beneficial for businesses, why haven't more companies adopted this technology? The greatest obstacles have been the costs associated with storing large quantities of data and the computing power required to process large-scale data, both of which have been removed by recent reductions in hardware costs and advances in technical capabilities. Another factor that has slowed the spread of data mining has been the lack of publicity about data mining success stories. Many companies consider their use of data mining as a way to gain significant competitive edge and are reluctant to divulge the secrets of their success. Finally, the perception that data mining is extremely complex and expensive has slowed its widespread adoption by the business community. Fortunately, software vendors have developed a variety of tools that have made data mining easier to deploy within an organization and easier to understand for business users who are not statisticians.

Data mining tasks can be generally categorized as **descriptive** or **predictive** depending on the type of business problem to be solved. Some data mining implementations will even use a combination of descriptive and predictive techniques. Descriptive data mining seeks to describe new patterns in the data and requires human interaction to determine the significance and meaning of these patterns. Examples of descriptive data mining tasks include **affinity grouping**, **clustering**, and **visualization**. Affinity grouping describes which items go together and is often used by retailers to plan product placement in their stores and by companies with many products to identify cross-selling opportunities. Clustering divides data into smaller groups based on similarity without predefinition of the groups and is often used to find customers with similar buying habits. Visualization provides a graphical representation of data that sometimes reveals patterns that are more apparent to the human eye than by other data mining approaches.

The alternative to descriptive data mining is predictive data mining, which is employed when available data is used to glean information that will automatically be applied to new data. The term *predictive* should not be taken literally, however, because data mining cannot really predict individual behavior; it can only point to the likelihood of a particular outcome. Nonetheless, results are often better than if no predictive data mining had been applied. In predictive data mining tasks, which include **classification** and **estimation**, mathematical algorithms are used to create models that best describe existing data. In classification a new record is assigned to a specific category defined by the model, such as classifying new credit applicants as low risk, medium risk, or high risk. An estimation task is used to assign a new record with a predicted value, such as the length of time a customer will stay.

Data mining often raises more questions than it answers, which is to be expected. These new questions can often be the starting point of a valuable top-down analysis. For this reason data mining and OLAP are increasingly implemented in tandem. For example, predicted values can be stored in an OLAP cube and made available for slicing and dicing. Several of the major database vendors are anticipating a rise in demand for this type of functionality and are integrating these technologies in their products.

The Data Warehouse

Now that you have some perspective on what reporting and analysis processes offer business users, we can turn our attention to understanding how a data warehouse fulfills the needs of a business. Because the primary job of the data warehouse is to support reporting and analysis, the requirements of the business drive its content and design. In practice this means that businesspeople define the information that will help them make better decisions faster so that IT professionals can build a data warehouse to meet their needs.

This practice is most successful when businesspeople and IT specialists share a common understanding of what a company's business requirements are and how a data warehouse fulfills these requirements. To help you gain and promote this understanding in your organization, we explain what a data warehouse looks like and how it can be used to fulfill a company's analysis requirements. (In Chapters 9 and 10 we describe how you can identify specific BI opportunities in your organization and how your company can embark on implementing a BI solution to take advantage of these opportunities.)

Common Characteristics

To develop a baseline understanding of what a data warehouse offers a company, let's explore some of its common characteristics by describing how a data warehouse stores business data.

Subject Oriented

As you learned earlier in the chapter, the data warehouse organizes data into subject-specific groups called data marts. These data marts are not individual silos of data like the operational source systems. Rather, data marts add value by being able to gather data from lots of operational systems to enable a specific line of analysis, such as a finance data mart that supports product line profitability. To present a cohesive source of data to business decision makers within an organization, data in the data warehouse is shared among the data marts.

Consistent Data

A data warehouse provides business users with a consistent set of data, that is, dimensions and measures. Consistent means that the data reported and analyzed has the same definitions across the data warehouse—and across the company at large. Achieving consistent data in a data warehouse requires a company to consider both data integration decisions and organizational decisions.

When source data comes from multiple operational systems, it is necessary to decide how you will integrate the data into one common view for analysis and reporting. For example, when you need to analyze the effects of discounts on profit margin, you notice that each of your company's source systems assigns a slightly different meaning to *discount*. A data warehouse presents the opportunity to integrate this disparate data based on a uniform understanding of how you want to report and analyze discounts. Another example is when source systems have slightly different dimensional data, such as organizational structures, product hierarchies, or geographic roll-ups. The data warehouse can also mitigate these differences in dimensional structures by defining uniform dimension designs.

Storing consistent data also requires you to make some organizational decisions regarding how you assign standardized meanings to the measures and dimensions within and between departments. For example, a sales department may need to decide how the metric sales revenue is calculated. Does sales revenue include only the direct sales of the company's sales representatives or does it also include indirect sales such as orders placed over the Internet? The company will certainly be interested in both flavors of sales revenue; the key is making sure that each flavor is clearly identified and universally agreed upon. Making sure that people in a company speak the same language in terms of dimensions and measures is critical to ensure that consistent reports are generated across the organization.

Cleansed Data

When business users report and analyze data from a data warehouse, they want cleansed data, that is, data that has been validated according to business and structural rules. The good news is that storing cleansed data is one of the data warehouse's most important priorities and business benefits. The bad news is that the source data from operational systems usually does not start out in a cleansed state. We call this uncleansed data **dirty data**.

Dirty data can be data that is missing, for example, the person who entered a cancellation order into the order entry system did not enter a reason why the customer cancelled the order. Dirty data is sometimes flat out incorrect data such as *Attttlanta, Georgia*—also typically the result of a data entry error. Dirty data can also be more subtle, such as sales orders that have been counted twice because of an error in the order entry system. To cleanse dirty data from the operational systems for storage in the data warehouse, ETL processes are used to load valid data and reject invalid data based on a company's business rules.

Historical Data

Being able to analyze data over specific periods of time is a powerful benefit of the data warehouse. Unlike operational systems, which focus on managing the day-to-day transactions of the business, a data warehouse is interested in providing business users with snapshots of data from the operational systems. These snapshots typically do not change from minute to minute like the operational systems. Rather, the data warehouse is refreshed with new snapshots of data in periodic intervals such as hours, days, weeks, or months. It is for this reason that data warehouses are considered to be nonvolatile (nonchanging). By storing these snapshots over time, business users can analyze and identify historical trends and exceptions in the data. For example, business users can compare how their product sales from the quarter of the current year compare to product sales from the same quarter last year and the year before.

Fast Delivery of Data

To support analysis at the speed of thought, a data warehouse must provide data to its business users in a timely and efficient manner. This means that the database technologies and the behind-the-scenes data structures need to support fast and efficient delivery of the data. Within the data warehouse architecture, there are two types of databases that are used to host data marts: OLAP databases and relational databases.

The benefits of OLAP databases were described in Chapter 2—their support of the multidimensional paradigm and fast data retrieval capabilities. Recall that we also explored a scenario where the task was to examine unit sales, average price, and amount sales for 100 products across 24 months of history for 100 customers in 20 districts. We estimated that this combination of parameters produced over 14 million values to consider. OLAP databases effectively handle all these data combinations because they preprocess the source transactions and save aggregated values in structures that are optimized for fast data retrieval. This makes OLAP databases great candidates for hosting data marts.

Although OLAP database technologies have been available for many years, more recently we have seen two important developments: the ease with which OLAP databases can be constructed has been greatly improved, and the cost of acquiring world-class OLAP databases has dropped dramatically. The combined effect of these two developments is that we are entering a new era of OLAP for the masses. The technology that once was available to only a select few people in the largest organizations is now available to all information consumers in even the smallest organizations.

Given the performance benefits of OLAP databases, you may wonder what role relational databases play in a data warehouse architecture. Within the data warehouse itself, the RDBMS is often used in conjunction with OLAP databases to host data marts, in some cases supplying data to the OLAP databases. In this scenario the RDBMS typically stores more detailed data than the OLAP database, which typically contains a summarized view of data. For example, to support sales analysis, a sales data mart may contain a relational component to host the detailed daily sales order data; it may also contain an OLAP component to store summarized sales data by customer, product, month, and region.

Relational databases can also host data marts in an independent role—without OLAP databases—by having their own set of dimensions and measures to support business reporting and analysis. Often this approach relies on using front-end tools to assemble the relational data into a business-friendly format and to provide the data to business users in a timely manner. In many cases, reporting from relational data marts requires the application of sophisticated front-end tools to make the data more understandable for business analysis.

Summary

The data warehouse architecture offers a flexible and effective decision-support framework for organizing and delivering data to business decision makers. It brings business intelligence to life through its usage of data warehouses, data marts, database technologies, ETL tools, and reporting and analysis tools—all working toward the single purpose of helping business-people make better decisions faster.

Business Intelligence Case Studies

To demonstrate the real-world application of business intelligence, the five case studies that compose Part II describe how companies across several industries successfully apply business intelligence to improve the quality of their decision making at various organizational levels.

Chapter 4 presents how *Audi AG,* the luxury performance arm of Volkswagen AG, uses business intelligence to improve the efficiency of its vehicle assembly line operations at its plant in Ingolstadt, Germany.

Chapter 5 portrays how the *Frank Russell Company,* a global investment services firm, applies business intelligence when taking action toward improving its revenues and product profitability.

Chapter 6 chronicles how *CompUSA,* America's largest computer superstore retailer, applies business intelligence to advance the day-to-day operations of the business through performance improvements, data quality enhancements, loss prevention, and productivity gains.

Chapter 7 recounts how *Disco SA,* a leading chain of supermarkets in Argentina, uses business intelligence to enhance the services and programs that keep customers loyal to the Disco brand.

Chapter 8 details how *Cascade Designs,* a privately held manufacturer of outdoor lifestyle products in Seattle, Washington, uses business intelligence to maintain a stable workforce in its highly seasonal industry by having the necessary information to perform superior production scheduling and inventory management.

Improving Operational Efficiency—Audi AG

Business intelligence has taken Audi in new directions in improving operational efficiency. We look forward to where it can take us in the future.
    —*Heinz Braun, Manager,* Fahrzeugsteuerung, *Audi AG*

Audi's maxim, "Vorsprung durch Technik" ("Progress Through Technology"), describes the German car manufacturer's legacy of pioneering advancements through the application of technology. When applied to business intelligence, the slogan describes how Audi has used technology to implement business intelligence at the core of its manufacturing efforts—the vehicle assembly line. To improve the efficiency of Audi's assembly line processes, the vehicle operations data mart (also known as the *Fahrzeugsteuerung* data mart) provides line managers at its assembly plant in Ingolstadt, Germany, with the necessary insight to successfully guide the day-to-day operations of the assembly line.

Company Background

The roots of Audi AG began in 1899 when August Horch founded his car manufacturing company in Cologne, Germany. Between 1899 and 1910, Horch successfully manufactured and distributed his first line of automobiles. In 1910, however, Horch left his company, Horch AG, after a fallout with the company business manager. After leaving, Horch had to start all over again but was restricted from using his surname to title any new enterprises. A friend's son cleverly suggested that Horch translate his last name to Latin. In German, "horch" is the imperative form of the verb "to listen." When translated to Latin, "horch" becomes "audi." With Audi as the name of his new enterprise, Horch chose an enduring epithet that has seized the attention of the automotive world for almost 100 years.

Case study information was collected through interviews conducted by dc soft Gmbh of Munich, Germany.

Audi is now one of the companies that form Volkswagen Aktiengesellschaft (AG). Since its inception in 1932, Volkswagen AG has risen to become the largest European car manufacturer and the third largest automaker in the world. Within the Volkswagen group, Audi has assumed the role of the luxury performance arm of the company, selling more than 650,000 Audi models in 2000, with sales revenues totaling more than DM 39 billion.

With a firm commitment to technological progress, safety, design, and premium vision, Audi looks for ways to improve its manufacturing efficiency, while continuing to produce superior cars with quality customer service. Because every car is "made on demand" (each car is manufactured according to specific customer requirements), Audi requires immediate intelligence of its assembly line operations to ensure on-time deliveries to its customers. Obtaining this intelligence in a timely manner introduces significant challenges from an operations perspective because managers must gather all the materials necessary to analyze how fluctuating customer demands impact the operation of the assembly line.

Business Requirements

Selling premium "made-on-demand" cars is a challenging business, especially from a data collection perspective. Rather than selling directly to customers, car manufacturers typically sell premium cars indirectly to customers through dealerships. While the car manufacturer can easily collect dealership data by tracking the vehicles sold to the dealers, it is more difficult to collect sell-through customer data from the dealers. This gap in data collection is often highlighted when a car manufacturer conducts a customer satisfaction survey.

Audi experienced this challenge in 1999 when it executed a worldwide customer satisfaction survey. To conduct the survey, Audi needed access to the customer sell-through information. With both a lack of centralization of customer and vehicle sales data and an archaic database technology, the entire process proved to be quite challenging, time-consuming, and costly. The work to organize this data fell on the shoulders of a few information technology (IT) professionals who spent months hunting down and assembling data from the dealerships.

Once the data was collected, Audi discovered that 95 percent of the customers interviewed in the survey would buy the same model again. Recognizing the potential value that this data offered, Audi realized that it needed better access to this information. Audi therefore committed to improving its sell-through data collection and analysis processes and concluded that it needed to increase its investments in business intelligence.

With this renewed commitment to business intelligence, Audi applied its motto ("Vorsprung durch Technik") to launch its BI initiatives. The first BI initiative arose in 1999 from the *Fahrzeugsteuerung* department of the Ingolstadt plant. This department is in charge of vehicle assembly line operations.

Successful operation of the assembly line requires complex process planning and line performance analysis to optimize throughput and quickly target and correct bottlenecks in the assembly line. Heinz Braun explains:

> Each workday is a unique 24 hours when you need to precisely coordinate suppliers, self-managing work crews, labor unions, and chains of command. Company-wide information systems must have up-to-date information to allow us to handle daily turbulences, to execute the utmost operational efficiency at any point in time, and to ensure that all our automobiles are built as desired.

To guide the operation of the assembly line, Audi uses simulation software from Rockwell Automation to plan upcoming production loads, sometimes several days in advance. The goal of the simulation is to analyze the upcoming productivity of the assembly line in order to uncover potential issues that could slow down throughput. Armed with this information, operations managers can quickly take corrective action to fix what is broken or to remove certain cars from the line before the actual assembly process begins.

To guide the assembly line, operations managers need to analyze hundreds of simultaneous measurements at various points in the assembly line from several different perspectives. For example, to ensure that the target throughput can be achieved for a given shift, operations managers need to view simulated car counts and issue counts by models, country customizations, versions, and sizes. When an issue arises that affects a vehicle's delivery time, such as an out-of-stock engine, managers need to know which customers ordered these vehicles so that they can notify each customer of the delivery delay. Issues can also be slightly more complicated when they affect multiple shifts on the assembly line. Because each shift is run by self-organized crews, any backlog in the assembly line needs to be communicated to the subsequent shift so that it can take corrective action—slow down, speed up, or remove certain cars from the line if the materials are not available.

In order to perform this type of analysis, operations managers historically created routines to extract and assemble information from the simulation data store. However, these operations managers often did not have the skills to develop the programs necessary to extract this data, which led to spending countless hours writing and debugging code with little results. When the data did arrive, it was often too late for the operations manager to impact the actual assembly line process.

The Solution

To meet these business requirements, the *Fahrzeugsteuerung* enlisted the help of external consultants who worked hand-in-hand with Audi operations managers to build the operations data mart.

One of the first steps in this process was to develop a flexible data model that could meet a line manager's analysis needs. This task was quite challenging because a single assembly line can build all types of a car model, from sedans to station wagons, with variations in country customizations, interior color, exterior color, seat upholstery, and many other features. To account for this complexity, the design of the data model has included more than 50 dimensions and hundreds of measurements.

To define and refine the data model, the implementation team built a prototype data mart for end users to explore. Part of this process involved choosing a back-end database engine and front-end analysis software to host the solution. The primary decision factors in choosing the host BI technology were low cost, high performance, and high manageability. Based on these criteria and to organize and manage the data, Audi selected the OLAP technology offered by Microsoft to produce a fast and flexible view of the simulation data. To provide operations managers with an easy-to-use data access interface, Audi chose ProClarity as the front-end reporting and analysis software to deliver the data stored in the OLAP database.

Once the technologies and initial design were determined, the next step was to understand the more sophisticated design challenges that the solution needed to handle for full deployment. One specific challenge was the timely extraction of data from the simulation data store to the OLAP database. To help extract and transform the data, the team used Data Transformation Services (DTS) to develop rerunable data load routines for loading data into the OLAP database. To provide the immediate intelligence that the managers required, the team used DTS to update the OLAP database in 60-minute increments.

Because they could sufficiently meet the immediate analysis requirements of the operations managers, the implementation team enhanced the design of the data mart to support long-term analysis needs. With this enhancement, the OLAP database now separately stores historical data to allow operations managers to perform trend and exception reporting of the assembly line over longer periods of time, such as weeks, months, and years.

Solution Benefits

By receiving hourly updates of simulated data, operations managers no longer need to rely on guesswork to guide the assembly line. Using interactive, online reports, such as the one in Figure 4-1, managers can view how many cars pass through various points in the assembly line by several different dimensions, such as model, color, time, and country customization.

An interactive report provides operations managers with immediate knowledge of how many cars are going through the production line, which customers are buying these cars, and how long it will take to move each car through every point in the assembly process. By having this information before the actual assembly process begins, operations managers can make the necessary adjustments to manage the vehicle production schedule from shift to shift. For example, if a particular options package is not available for a special vehicle, all cars that require this package will be removed from the line and rescheduled for another day. When rescheduling impacts the vehicle delivery time frame, the customer is promptly notified of any delays.

The ability to take corrective action before the actual assembly line process begins has brought Audi into a new era of cost savings and operational efficiency. No longer are operations managers looking for a needle in a haystack or depending on guesswork to manage the assembly line. With simulated data at their fingertips, they can effectively take charge of the assembly line and steer its operations with greater certainty and relative ease.

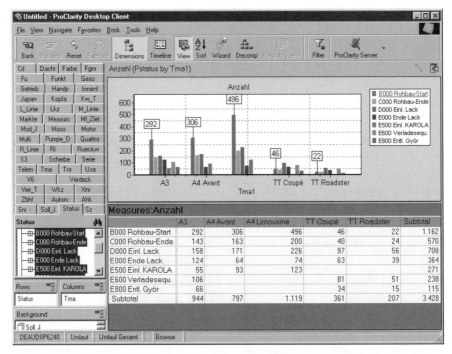

Figure 4-1.   *A sample interactive report for Audi operations managers*

Future Plans

With the *Fahrzeugsteuerung* data mart successfully guiding assembly line operations, future plans include implementing a data mart to measure the actual performance of the active assembly line. By centralizing simulated and actual data, analysts will be able to view both types of data side by side, thereby allowing them to easily measure variances and uncover trends. With a complete picture of the relationships between simulated and actual processes, Audi can pursue more aggressive order-to-delivery time frames and provide its customers with more flexibility to make last-minute changes to vehicle orders.

The information from the data mart also has the potential to be leveraged by other departments in the company. For example, the research and development department can use this information to evaluate new designs, make upgrade decisions, and target new areas of development based on the performance of the assembly line. This information can also be used to enhance customer service initiatives in the sales and marketing departments, such as learning which colors, models, and other variations are selling well or poorly.

Summary

With the success of the *Fahrzeugsteuerung* data mart, operation managers have made significant improvements in the efficiency of their assembly line processes. By having flexible access to the simulation data, operation managers now have the ability to quickly identify potential supplier, assembly, and design issues and to take swift corrective action before the actual assembly line process begins.

With future plans to share this information with other departments, the data mart enables Audi to understand how production information can be integrated with other business units to enhance its customer service. This initial success coupled with Audi's proven motto suggests that there are no limitations to what Audi can achieve with business intelligence.

Maximizing Profitability—The Frank Russell Company

Demand for additional reports became increasingly overwhelming.
Delivery of one report in response to one question invariably led to another
question and a request for a new report, but processing these requests was
taking too long. We needed to empower users with direct, interactive access
to the data. We wanted something that anybody could learn quickly and
could use to satisfy his or her unique data analysis needs. With Picasso and
Einstein, we achieved this goal.

—Matt Knox, Director of Data Resource Management,
the Frank Russell Company

Monitoring the daily flow of mutual fund and stock trades is critical to the
operations of the Frank Russell Company. Through two key BI initiatives,
code-named Picasso and Einstein, analysts and managers of the mutual fund
operations and institutional brokerage units can now access information
more quickly to make decisions and take action toward improving revenues
and product profitability.

Company Background

Russell is one of the world's leading investment managers, with assets under
management (AUM) of more than $66 billion. Some of the largest institu-
tional investors around the world turn to Russell to guide the investment of
over $1 trillion worldwide, while more than 40 million individual investors
have access to Russell's services through its alliances with leading banks,
brokers, insurance companies, and independent investment advisors.

Case study information was collected through interviews conducted by Aspirity, LLC, of
Bellevue, Washington.

The company was founded as a small brokerage firm in 1936 by Frank Russell in Tacoma, Washington. In 1999 it became a subsidiary of Northwestern Mutual, a leader in the life insurance and financial services industries. Today, Russell employs more than 1300 people in nine offices around the world and generates annual revenues of $500 million. In 2002 the company was ranked 11th in the nation in *Fortune* magazine's annual list of the "100 Best Companies to Work for in America."

Continuous in-depth research by investment managers and extensive knowledge of capital markets have enabled Russell to develop a 360-degree perspective of the financial marketplace, which provides a complete view of money management options for its investors. Not only can the right blend of investment managers be selected to achieve specific investment goals, but an understanding of the markets, issues, and regulatory environments around the world is used to make intelligent selections of regional and global funds. Russell is now bringing that same perspective to its internal operations through the deployment of business intelligence. Having a 360-degree internal view provides the company with new insights into the trends that affect its bottom line.

Business Requirements

Recognizing that access to timely information is crucial to managing day-to-day operations, Russell had already established an environment in which each business unit could independently retrieve data and analyze the prior day's trade transactions. Business users had access to predefined tabular reports in which they could make simple changes, such as specifying date ranges or selecting specific funds. However, with ever-changing market conditions, new business questions about the potential impact on projected revenues emerged constantly. Analysts needed quick responses to these questions to take the action necessary to protect revenues as best as possible, but the predefined reports did not go far enough to support these needs. A better solution was essential to moving the business forward.

To improve information access, a designated analyst within each business unit was trained to use query and reporting tools, such as Microsoft Access and Cognos Impromptu. These analysts could use these tools to create reports as needed to answer questions on demand, instead of relying on canned reports. Since this information was often delivered as a printed report, the person asking for the information could not manipulate the data or enhance it with additional information without returning to the analyst with a request for yet another report. This continual cycle of report production to respond to a series of questions became increasingly time-consuming and often resulted in the information arriving too late for a requestor to take action.

Recognizing that a better solution was essential, Matthew Knox, the Director of Data Resource Management, and his team first considered building a traditional data warehouse environment for reporting purposes. After reviewing the reporting requirements, they realized that a way to support both transaction-level details and summary information was part of the goal. To build this support into the data warehouse, they would have to know in advance what combinations of information should be summarized, but this would only solve part of the problem—getting information to known questions to the analysts faster. To solve the additional problem of answering new questions quickly, they had the daunting task of anticipating every likely combination of information that could be summarized and building these summaries into the warehouse. There was no way to know which combinations would be worth the effort.

After attending an introductory presentation on OLAP technology, Knox believed he could finally resolve the reporting issue problems by enabling business users to quickly and easily find the answers they were seeking through self-directed data exploration. "With OLAP, we could have a more flexible environment. Every summary you could think of is already built in," Knox explains. The mutual funds operations unit already had a well-appreciated business need to provide better access to the data, and after Knox explained his idea, they agreed to fund a research project as a proof of concept.

The goal of the project was to build a prototype, with data from the mutual fund operations unit, to confirm that OLAP was the ideal solution. Using tools already in-house, Knox combined the reporting capabilities of Cognos with the OLAP functionality included in Microsoft SQL Server to create a BI solution with no additional software costs. To assist with the project, Knox brought in a BI consulting firm. "It's not that the technology is difficult, but it was worthwhile to bring in outside help to save time in learning."

The completed prototype demonstrated that when the data was placed in OLAP cubes, the structure made sense to the business users and was easy to use for building reports. By leveraging the design work performed as part of the prototype, Knox was confident in the success of the future project because "it was clear after the proof of concept that it would be useful, and we were already partway down the path." When he showed Russell executives his plan, he won their sponsorship to launch the Picasso project in early 2000.

The Picasso Solution

The goal of the Picasso project was to build a system to allow business users to interactively analyze mutual fund trades. To meet the need of having access to the most current information possible, a process runs every night to extract the trade transactions that occurred during the day, as well as changes to earlier transactions, from a fund management system stored in Sybase Adaptive Server Enterprise. This data is loaded into a Microsoft SQL Server relational database, where it is organized for updates to three OLAP cubes designed especially for analyzing daily trades and transactions by account and the current month's running totals for each account. Figure 5-1 illustrates the Picasso architecture.

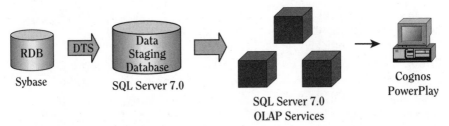

Figure 5-1. *Picasso architecture*

Business users are now able to analyze trends in cash flow, assets under management, and fund activity. As a starting point, they access an intranet page designed for Picasso, with reports containing tabular data and charts. For example, an analyst can select a report to study AUM by business relationship and then probe further by reviewing the market value of the funds on a monthly and year-to-date basis. Deeper analysis can be performed by drilling into the data to see details for a selected channel, such as advisors, and even more specifically for a specific office or representative.

Casual business users, typically managers, access reports with a Web browser using the company intranet, while other users with more advanced reporting needs use the full client version of Cognos PowerPlay. Users often start with the Web version of the Cognos tools to explore an idea. If the results are useful, the user gives the report to the designated analyst who enhances the report in the full client version to add additional formatting and other features. The final version of the report is then published on the intranet site to make it available for interactive analysis by other users in the business unit, as illustrated in Figure 5-2. This blend of technology, skills, and shared business insight enables Russell to continuously leverage its BI investment.

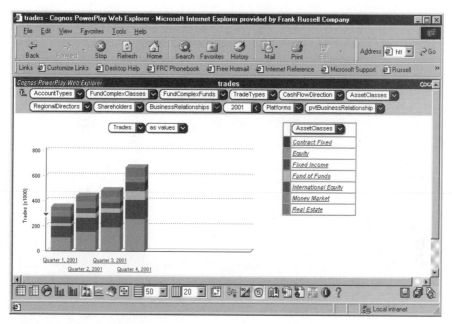

Figure 5-2.   *Sample Picasso report*

Solution Benefits

One of the benefits of Picasso is a reduction in the time spent gathering operational data. Before its implementation, the process to gather, summarize, and distribute the previous day's transactions took until 2 P.M., but now everyone has access to this information within the first five minutes of the workday.

The time required to develop a new report has also improved radically. Shortly after Picasso was implemented, a manager asked an analyst for a report on a new fund since its inception and expected the report to be delivered hours later. Within two minutes, the manager had the requested information in hand.

More complex reports obviously require more time, but with effective business intelligence in place, the turnaround time has been greatly reduced, according to Eric Espinal, Data Specialist.

> For example, our sales unit wanted to monitor cash flow activity for 300 representatives for a specified time period. Before business intelligence, we would most likely have used Microsoft Access to query various tables on Sybase. This process would have taken approximately 2–3 hours to build and about 20 minutes to run the queries. With business intelligence, we were able to create the same process in about 30 minutes, and running the report takes just seconds. In addition to just reporting cash flow, we were able to identify which funds were selling, view their AUM balance across various time periods, and view selling trends.

Most importantly, each business user has direct and faster access to the data needed to support individual decision making. Rod Greenshields, Product Analyst in the Product Development and Management unit, explains:

> Picasso is an invaluable tool because it provides me with access to data that would otherwise be inaccessible or laborious to obtain. The basic Picasso reports offer an easy way to quickly examine such things as cash flow and AUM statistics, with the ability to always drill down deeper and analyze that information from a number of perspectives, such as by distribution channel or fund share class. Picasso makes me seem smarter by helping me answer questions that leave others stumped.

A key contributor to Picasso's success was the ability to rapidly prototype the solution. According to Knox, "We produced, literally in a few days, something the users could see. The value of this project was readily apparent as soon as the users' own data was put in front of them." As the project developed, the historic information in the prototype stabilized, and users began using it for their reports. Knox says, "Ordinarily we measure success by the sign-off on a project by the business sponsor. In this case we recognized our success early—as soon as users started using the prototype."

Involving users early on also helped to get buy-in for the project and ensured that the design supported their requirements. Through several iterative cycles, users would participate in a requirements session to define needed dimensions. The implementation team would build a test cube with a few dimensions at a time, and then users would experiment with the results and return with requests for more dimensions. According to Knox, "The project had a limit on the number of dimensions that would be supported. We tried to follow the **80/20 rule** regarding which dimensions would be the most valuable initially."

Using a Web-based client tool has also been very effective and ensures a new user can be successful with minimal training. "If a person can use e-mail, he or she can use these tools," Knox says. "Just a few minutes of training and let 'em go!"

The Einstein Solution: Building on Success

After the success of Picasso, the IT department at Russell saw an opportunity to do some internal marketing to find leads for another BI solution. In many ways, Russell's IT department is similar to a consulting organization because the various business units are charged for services rendered, and IT must seek out interested internal "clients" when it has a new capability that could be useful. Through informal forums established at Russell to share knowledge and best practices, the institutional brokerage business unit learned about OLAP from Picasso users. The unit was eager to use OLAP, and armed with a good business case, it engaged IT to help launch the next BI project, known as Einstein.

The institutional brokerage business unit planned to use Einstein to improve its ability to manage product profitability and vendor relationships. The unit already had a designated analyst using Cognos Impromptu to develop analytical reports, but the information that management continually requested was difficult to obtain and complex to compile without involving IT. To respond to these questions on demand would incur a cost each time from IT, with no guarantee that the results could be reused in the future. Without knowing what the results would be once the numbers could be pulled together, the managers of the institutional brokerage business unit could not justify the expense required. Instead of gathering the hard evidence they could use during vendor negotiations, they chose instead to operate from gut feelings. "There was no way to value the information before you could see it," explains Knox.

Once Einstein was implemented, business users had access to information that was previously unobtainable and were delighted with the results. Managers could now quantify the value of their decisions with minimal effort. Best of all, a one-time investment in a BI solution could be extended across multiple decision-making activities. The project's sponsor remarked, "The project was completed on time and under budget, and it delivered exactly what was promised."

Einstein was launched in May 2001 to support the analysis of revenue from trades performed on behalf of money managers and to study product profitability. The project was less complex than Picasso and required a smaller team to implement. Nonetheless, to guarantee success, one of the consultants from Picasso returned on a part-time basis over a period of five months to assist the database administrator assigned to the project.

In this implementation, the transactional data as well as the analysis goals were substantially different from Picasso, so previous design work could not be reused. With Picasso, users need to monitor and respond to the flow of daily mutual fund trades, but with Einstein, users need to review sales of financial products with an eye on overall profitability. However, the technology platform, a combination of Microsoft and Cognos tools, was already proven and could be easily extended for this project. Just as with Picasso, timeliness of data is a major requirement for Einstein users, so a similar nightly process is run to extract the day's trade transactions from a Sybase database and loaded into its own Microsoft SQL Server relational and OLAP database.

Brokerage analysts, using Web-based or full-client Cognos tools, are now able to study share volume; the number of trades; commissions along with averages; per share information; and comparisons to the prior year for any combination of brokers, managers, and fund and manager representatives, as well as an array of funds.

Solution Benefits

Company executives are now able to prepare thoroughly for negotiations with vendors. With accurate and easily obtained information, managers can identify which vendors are receiving high volumes of business and use this knowledge to successfully negotiate more favorable discounts on trade commissions. Thomas Morton, Director of Relationship Sales at Frank Russell Securities, adds:

> Einstein has allowed Frank Russell Securities to better manage vendors by providing access to information ratios on our business. In particular, we have been able to quickly query the data during a live phone conversation to better support our negotiating position.
>
> Additionally, Einstein has opened the door for ongoing analysis of our business. We are now able, in a timely manner, to analyze the ebb and flow of our business across services, regions, clients, pricing, currencies, and market factors. This information gives us the ability to adapt quickly to replicate our successes as well as avoid our failures. This data and analysis have become critical elements in properly managing our business. The velocity of our business is accelerating, and fortunately, so are the tools with which we manage it.

Summary

The Frank Russell Company has successfully deployed two BI solutions in 2000 and 2001 and plans to expand these deployments to include European and Asian data sources to bring a global perspective to its internal operations.

Picasso has removed the barriers to quick and easy access to information for the mutual fund operations unit, giving managers and analysts more time to act on information coming from a marketplace of rapidly changing conditions. The speed with which they are able to study the impact of negative trends allows them to respond proactively and protect the bottom line through improved revenue management.

Einstein, too, has made its share of contributions to the bottom line. Brokerage managers can easily and independently assess the relative value of vendor relationships and trading volumes and take decisive action to maximize profitability.

Impacting the Bottom Line—CompUSA Inc.

The data warehouse has simplified data access for general managers, individuals who run retail operations and work very long hours. They work seven days a week. They don't have a lot of time to go in and dump data to an Excel spreadsheet. So the real goal is to make the data simple and concise, summarize it, and show them the exceptions so they can go fix it.
—Cathy Witt, Vice President and Chief Information Officer, CompUSA

For CompUSA, its Business Analytics Data Warehouse brings together information from each retail location to provide a consistent view of sales for each individual store and consolidated reports at regional, divisional, and corporate levels. Having this consistency ensures that the direction set by senior management is clearly communicated to store-level management, which in turn leads to a common understanding of the actions to be taken and enables the desired results to be achieved.

From day-to-day decision making to strategic initiatives, the Business Analytics Data Warehouse at CompUSA has empowered store managers and corporate executives to gain the insight they need to better manage productivity and profits.

Company Background

CompUSA Inc. has undergone several name and operational transformations since it launched its business in 1984 as Soft Warehouse in Dallas, Texas. The company originally sold directly to business customers, prior to opening its first retail store in 1985 and its first computer superstore in 1988. Soft Warehouse became CompUSA in 1991. The Mexican retail company Grupo Sanborns then acquired CompUSA in March 2000. Throughout its

---

Case study information was collected through interviews conducted by Microsoft Corporation, Redmond, Washington.

history, the company has continued its growth through expansion and acquisitions to become the largest computer retailer in North America, with 225 computer superstores in 84 metropolitan markets and a virtual computer superstore on its corporate Web site for online shoppers around the world.

While retail is still at the core of each CompUSA store and the corporate Web site, the stores now have branched into other areas, such as corporate sales services, classroom training, and a variety of technical services. "Even though our name still says computer superstore, we've begun to evolve into more of a technology company as opposed to a computer company," says Steve Ellison, Senior Director of Store Operations.

As with classic retail businesses, CompUSA measures its performance by monitoring sales, margins, and profitability. However, the company differentiates itself from its competitors, who typically sell a variety of electronics, appliances, and other goods, by focusing exclusively on selling technology products and services. This focus enables the company not only to provide superior customer service but also continually to find ways to leverage technology and improve the way CompUSA manages its business.

Business Requirements

The store operations management team spans the organization and includes the general manager of each store, regional managers, divisional managers, and corporate executives. Because the results of the previous day's sales drive the actions of this team, each day previously began with sales analysis reports available from legacy systems. These reports provided limited information, such as sales, margin, and quantity of sell-through, for each product sold on the previous day for each store. Comparisons of raw sales and profitability between stores and regions were possible, but the legacy system could not provide details about the daily activities that affect a store's performance, such as discretionary discounting at each store, missed opportunities to sell extended warranties, or a cashier's failure to capture complete warranty information. Managers needed access to this type of information so that they could implement corrective measures and monitor the results.

Management was also unable to use the sales information from legacy systems to effectively plan for the future. Management needed to understand more than just what products were selling, such as relationships inside each store, including how certain products were selling as compared to other products and which products were selling together. In addition, an ability to compare stores across the country would help management understand what mix of products sold at a store with a relatively high margin as compared to a store with a low margin. By understanding these differences, management could use this knowledge to take action to improve margins at all stores.

An obstacle to collecting information was the disparate point-of-sale systems in place within each store. Point-of-sale systems include devices, typically cash registers, which capture sales information at the time of purchase, such as product number and quantity, and the software used for locating product prices, calculating taxes and totals, and storing the transaction details. CompUSA's corporate sales, training, and technology services each had business exceptions that the retail point-of-sale systems could not accommodate. For example, training can be sold to an individual who wants to attend a standard instructor-led class or to an organization that wants an instructor to come on-site to provide several employees with training on the same software package. A traditional point-of-sale system is oriented around discrete product sales, so it cannot capture the type of sales information applicable to training services. As a result, separate systems were built or purchased for training and each of the other service businesses, which in some cases varied from store to store. CompUSA needed to centrally manage these information systems and to bring the data from these systems together to get one view of a customer, regardless of whether the sales came from retail, corporate sales, technical services, or the training business.

As the economy softened in 2000, the need to consolidate information across a store and to monitor sales hour by hour, and minute by minute, became even more critical. The legacy systems could not provide this level of detail nor was the data available between days. Management needed timely access to this information to give them the necessary edge to increase retail sales at each store, especially when big promotions were running.

The idea behind the Business Analytics Data Warehouse was to provide a solution to respond to these needs by providing a centralized repository for detailed sales information and the flexibility for the user to tailor reports to get different views of the information. With this infrastructure in place, CompUSA expected to boost sales through better management of sales personnel and to reduce losses resulting from rejected warranty claims and fraud through better collection of information at the time of sale.

According to Dennis Naherny, Director of Enterprise Data Management,

The goal of the first phase of our implementation was to provide some reporting to our store operations team, which included our general managers, our regional managers, and some key corporate executives. This was really a reporting of past sales history on a daily basis and an analysis of some trends and key business areas.

At each level, the scope of information visible to the business user would change according to the user's role in the organization. The general manager in every store, who is responsible for both retail and service sales, would need to receive a defined set of reports available about that store's performance by line of business. At the next level in the organization, regional managers would be able to see the same reports as general managers, but they would receive a more summarized view of the multiple stores they manage. Above the regional managers are the senior director of operations and two divisional vice presidents who would need similar reports with a view of the entire country.

The Solution

The technical team at CompUSA was very experienced with OLTP systems but needed to bring in data warehousing expertise to help them learn how to build and maintain the system. Three consultants were engaged in April 2001 to model the data, design the architecture for the staging and OLAP databases, design the stored procedures that move the data between databases, and design the Web architecture.

Over the next month, the team worked with store managers to define the reporting requirements for their business. Two key performance indicators—sales performance and profit contribution by product—were selected as the primary focus of the first phase. Two additional consultants joined the team in May 2001 to help with data transformation tasks and report development. Within three months the requirements analysis was complete, and a prototype was ready for review by regional and store managers.

Once feedback from management was incorporated into the design, an iterative approach was taken to building the data warehouse. The team started by pulling data from a single store to populate the data warehouse. After all the components of the architecture were successfully tested with this set of data, the team took the next step by pulling data from all stores within a region and combining it in the data warehouse. Step by step, additional regions were added to the data warehouse, resulting in the successful consolidation of sales data for the entire company.

The process to gather data and consolidate data is now performed on a daily basis in the hours during which an individual store is closed. The data is captured from the point-of-sale devices in the store early each morning and stored in a proprietary transaction log format that is collected at corporate headquarters. Omni Parser, a software product from Matra Systems, reads the logs and parses the data into a format that can be stored in a Microsoft SQL Server data warehouse. Accounting data from the legacy system is also integrated so that correct gross margins can be calculated. OLAP cubes hosted in a Microsoft SQL Server Analysis Services database then aggregate the sales data and filter it according to who is accessing the information.

Within each store, up to four managers have access to information through the corporate intranet using the Web version of ProClarity, a front-end analysis tool. According to Anna Halbert, General Manager of the Arlington, Texas, store,

> I can look at all the stores for the sales, gross margin, and services. Then I can isolate my store and look at all the sales by individual or by team members and know exactly what they sold. I can isolate almost any store and see how I did in comparison to them and take action after that.

Ellison explained the new approach to daily analysis:

> We have a daily report called "The Tracker" [Figure 6-1] that captures a half dozen key metrics that senior management wants to look at every day—the major drivers of our business. An executive can look at the company and drill into the regions and examine sales, sales to plan, margin percent, and similar types of metrics to look for anomalies. We're looking for the top two or three and the bottom two or three.

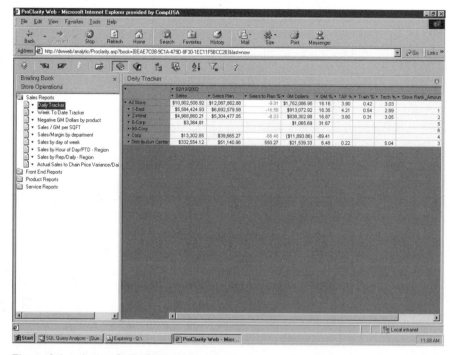

Figure 6-1. *A sample Daily Tracker report*

With the top performers identified, an executive can call the manager
and ask what is happening to drive the business. Conversely, the bottom performers can get the attention they need to get back on track. Whether a
region is doing well or poorly can be directly attributed to the performance
of just a few stores. "The ability to drill fairly quickly into store detail from
the executive tracker level is a very valuable tool that we just haven't had.
We haven't had the flexibility and the robustness to do this before."

Solution Benefits

After completing the first phase of implementation, the benefits of the
Business Analytics Data Warehouse have become readily apparent across all
levels of the organization. Access to information has enabled management to
take specific steps to improve the day-to-day operations of the business
through performance improvements, data quality improvements, loss prevention, and productivity gains.

Improved Sales Performance

The most visible benefit of the solution is the ability to associate a salesperson to each item sold in a single transaction. According to Landon West, General Manager of the Dallas, Texas, store,

> The data warehouse has enabled us to help the team perform better. Typically, salespeople will have data denial, so it has really enabled me to take a piece of paper with their sales information, point it out to them, and help them become more successful.

Improved Data Quality

Witt, CompUSA's Chief Information Officer, said, "The second benefit has been for our Technical Assurance Program, where we sell warranty on products. We are now collecting good customer information as well as serial number by product." Previously, sales personnel were not consistently capturing all customer information for the warranty program. Now the system allows store managers to identify which sales personnel are not collecting the required information and to take action to reduce the instances where CompUSA honors a warranty that was not collectable from the insurance company.

Fraud and Loss Prevention

Witt identifies the third main benefit as resolution of "the issues related to fraud and loss prevention because of the detail now available from the point-of-sale devices." Some customers falsely claim that they have a warranty on a product purchased from the company. Before the data warehouse, CompUSA did not have accurate data about warranties sold. The company elected to honor most claims, which resulted in significant losses. With better supervision of warranty sales, the company is in a better position to turn down unsubstantiated claims and minimize these losses.

Improved Productivity

Having a data warehouse that centralizes CompUSA's business data has replaced laborious, manual processes performed by different groups to gather data from multiple databases and put the data into spreadsheets. IT personnel are no longer spending time finding and integrating data from different sources in response to questions from business users. Managers are able to focus on analyzing data and acting on the information without spending time searching for the data and consolidating it into a usable form. Business analysts can also spend less time collecting data and instead spend more time developing plans to increase sales and decrease costs, which then contributes to increased profits. According to Naherny, "We believe that in one instance we may have saved up to three or four hours a week per team member to provide some weekly reporting for the executive management team."

Project Challenges

By phasing in the implementation of the Business Analytics Data Warehouse, the project team could limit its risks. Even so, there were challenges related to data volumes, data integration, and data quality, which the team had to resolve quickly in order to keep on schedule.

Data Volumes

With 10 million transactions per month, the volume of data that the data warehouse had to support was already large and growing. Through incremental prototyping, the team was able to demonstrate Microsoft SQL Server's ability to scale and perform with high data volumes on a regular basis. The ProClarity server, which serves as a middle tier, provides users access to the OLAP cubes; however, it did require some customization, with the help of the vendor, to handle high data volumes.

Data Integration

A common challenge in a data warehouse project is the integration of data from disparate source systems. In order to correctly calculate certain metrics, such as gross margins, CompUSA needed to combine accounting information with retail data from point-of-sale systems. Considerable time was spent validating the data between the previous sales analysis system and the new data warehouse. To keep the project moving while this ongoing reconciliation was taking place, compensating entries were made in the data warehouse to keep the systems in balance until discrepancies could be resolved.

Data Quality

Naherny pointed out: "Sometimes our stores don't always collect information accurately. Sometimes because of our legacy systems, and the fact that we have interface issues, we lose data in the translation process." The decision was made to leave the data alone so that senior management could see the poor quality of the data and help drive new processes to improve data collection in the stores.

Lessons Learned

Key to the ongoing success of the data warehouse is the plan to deliver results in 60–90 day increments. With the first phase of the project, the prototype was available within 90 days and was quickly followed by a roll-out of the system over the next 90 days. Witt explained: "We didn't lose the focus or the attention of the business because we could move fairly quickly.

Reflecting on the successful completion of the first phase of the project, Witt said,

> I think we had a very cohesive team. All of the business partners came together and put together a plan. We had to rework some of it since our volume was larger than anticipated because this was retail data and the transaction volume was very large, but it was a really good team. They worked through performance testing and all of that before the business came onto the system.

Future Plans

The success of the first phase of the data warehouse has paved the way for future expansion. According to Witt,

> We are about to go live with our second phase.... We are looking to possibly get back as much as $6 million, which would be over the next year's time frame, but it more than pays for the original implementation, the hardware investment, and the consulting.

> In the second phase, sales from the corporate Web site and small business channels will be included in the data warehouse.

The second phase moves CompUSA another step closer to its plan to bring together data from all areas of the business to get to a single view of the customer. By deploying analytical capabilities to the advertising and marketing teams, integrating the results of **click-stream analysis** from the corporate Web site, and implementing a customer loyalty program, CompUSA hopes to better understand who its customers are. With this type of information, the behavior of customers can be understood, and the company can take steps to enhance customer service opportunities.

Improving inventory management is another area for which the data warehouse will be enhanced over the next year. Naherny explained:

> We might be able to reduce our inventory or change our product mix, even on a small percentage basis. That could mean a savings of hundreds of thousands of dollars over the coming year.

Ultimately, the goal is to provide near real-time analysis to get a complete and timely picture of sales into the hands of store managers. Implementation of the data warehouse has brought CompUSA closer to realizing this goal. In the fall of 2001, a major promotion, Midnight Madness, was timed with the release of Microsoft Windows XP. As part of this promotion, the stores were open additional hours, from midnight until 2 A.M. Just five hours later, executives were able to see the sales results, which never would have been possible with the legacy systems. To take the next step, CompUSA is considering extending information access to handheld devices so that managers can walk around the store and use the information to work with cashiers and sales staff on an up-to-the-minute basis to improve performance.

Summary

In a six-month period, CompUSA was able to take mountains of data that was inaccessible at a practical level and transform it into information that executives and managers could use on a daily basis. Actions can now be taken not only to reverse the effect of downward trends but also to reinforce practices that lead to increased sales and improved margins. As CompUSA continues to expand the capabilities of the Business Analytics Data Warehouse, the net result will be a stronger bottom line for the company and a superior experience for its customers.

Keeping Customers Loyal—Disco S.A.

The data mining processes allow us to create more business value through the adoption of several actions—such as tailoring communications to each profile or undertaking specific promotions for interest groups—on the grounds of the new business knowledge we are obtaining.
—Horacio Diaz, Data Warehousing Project Leader, Disco S.A.

Providing its patrons with quality customer service has always been the key to success for Disco S.A, the leading supermarket chain in Argentina. To realize this corporate goal, Disco's BI initiatives continue to produce valuable insights into customer relationships, such as how promotional campaigns affect the purchasing behavior of customers and what characteristics describe the most loyal customers. Armed with these insights, decision makers across multiple departments—pricing, marketing, accounting, and merchandising—are able to continually add and enhance the services and programs that keep customers loyal to the Disco brand.

Company Background

Disco S.A. is known across Argentina for its supermarket chains, convenience stores, and private-label products. The company was founded there in 1961 and has been growing ever since. Disco is now a leader in the Argentine marketplace, with more than 230 locations, over 16,000 employees, and annual sales revenues of U.S.$2,047 million in 2000.

Disco attributes its success to the attention paid to the details that ensure a customer will want to return again and again. From an upscale shopping experience in its supermarkets to an online virtual store providing home delivery, the company relies on innovation to attract and retain its

---

Case study information was collected through interviews conducted by Microsoft Corporation, Buenos Aires, Argentina.

customers. Disco introduced in 1996 a frequent buyer program, DiscoPlus, which provides its members with exclusive offers and special services. The program has proven to be enormously successful for the company and now has over two million members enrolled.

Business Requirements

The DiscoPlus program not only rewards repeat customers but also provides Disco's business decision makers with a valuable resource for identifying and enhancing customer service opportunities. To access the information collected through the DiscoPlus program, business users were historically dependent on IT to provide information coming from online transaction systems, which consisted of synchronized servers in each region of Argentina in which Disco operated. To support statistical analysis about customer behavior, operational data was extracted from these servers to create a small OLAP cube using Pilot solutions from Accrue Software. IT used the cube to develop statistical reports with Microsoft Visual FoxPro; the reports were then converted to text files or Microsoft Excel spreadsheets and distributed to business users. While this process provided important customer sales information to business users, the users continued to be dependent on IT to prepare and distribute reports. Such a process could not be scaled to accommodate widespread user access to ever-growing volumes of customer data.

Not only was access to customer data limited in scope and format, but the timeliness of the information was also equally limited. Reports used frequently could only be refreshed with new data on a weekly basis. In addition, creating a new report from the online transactions systems often took several hours to produce and always required the involvement of IT resources. This delay in receiving information proved to be quite limiting to business users who, according to Diaz, "wanted more analytical, faster, and reliable information."

With this challenge in hand, Disco embarked on creating an effective BI solution to meet the information requirements of its decision makers and analysts. To support its efforts, Disco has long valued state-of-the-art technology, as evidenced by a technology investment plan that has been in place for several years. When IT suggested that the implementation of a data warehouse could resolve data access issues and better meet the information needs of business decision makers, the executive management at Disco agreed to support the effort. The driving force behind the data warehouse was a desire to understand the behavior of loyal customers so that the company could retain existing customers and attract new ones by developing products and services tailored to the customer. According to Carlos Ocaranza, leader of the resulting data warehouse team at Disco, the benefits of the data warehouse project were "easy for them [executive management] to understand because they already knew that technology, when applied to business needs, is critical for the success of our business."

The Solution

Given the potential business value of the data collected through the DiscoPlus program, the data warehouse team focused its efforts on meeting the business needs of the department that could extract immediate benefit from frequent buyer information—the marketing department. Specifically, the marketing department could use the detailed customer data to support the analytical studies associated with Disco's customer relationship management activities.

To address the analysis needs of the marketing department, the team examined the functionality of both OLAP and data mining technologies. The team found that OLAP technology would be best suited for the recurring analysis performed by the marketing department—answering known questions by navigating from the summary to detailed data. While OLAP technology seemed appropriate for some of their analysis needs, the team concluded that data mining technology would help the marketing department find previously unknown patterns in detailed data, patterns that could prove to be of significant business value. The data warehouse team consequently decided that the data warehouse would need to support data mining of the DiscoPlus data and would need to be directly accessible by business users for performing their own online analysis. With the goals of the project clearly defined, the team was ready to begin work.

The next step in the project required identification of the appropriate data sources so that the necessary data could be extracted from several sources and loaded into the data warehouse, which was hosted in a Microsoft SQL Server database. Generic sales data was collected from the point-of-sale systems for storage in the data warehouse on a daily basis. Additional data was available from the DiscoPlus program, which associates the items of each purchase with specific buyers. Finally, general information about Disco stores and products and customer data, collected when individuals enroll in the DiscoPlus program, were added to the data warehouse to provide the range and depth of detail needed for a successful data mining project.

With the data collected and organized for data mining, the data warehouse team selected the appropriate data mining technique to meet the analysis needs of the marketing department. When applying data mining to address specific business needs, the team analyzed two distinct categories of data mining techniques: descriptive data mining and predictive data mining. Descriptive data mining finds patterns in data to explain behavior, such as finding nonintuitive combinations of products commonly purchased together. Predictive data mining finds patterns that are used to identify trends, such as finding characteristics of customers who are likely to buy a particular product. Because the marketing department's main business need was to understand the behavior of loyal customers, the data warehouse team could narrow its choice to descriptive data mining techniques.

In particular, the data warehouse team used a combination of descriptive data mining techniques: segmentation and clustering. Segmentation put customers into distinct groups based on the frequency of purchase, the amount of time since a member's last purchase, and the size of each customer's purchase. This information would then be combined with additional facts about each customer from the DiscoPlus enrollment data, such as name, age, gender, marital status, occupation, number of children, and so forth. The clustering technique evaluated each segmented group of customers to find the common characteristics of each group. The results of using these techniques meant that the marketing department would be able to see the relationships between customer demographics and positive customer behavior, such as large and frequent purchases, and use this information to more effectively tailor promotional campaigns.

With the appropriate data mining techniques identified, the team selected the data mining and OLAP capabilities of Microsoft SQL Server Analysis Services to host the BI solution. To build the data mining model in Analysis Services, the team first created an OLAP cube to store the source data from the data warehouse. After creating the source OLAP cube, the data warehouse team selected the analysis technique to be applied, such as clustering, and the level of detail, such as individual customer, to be analyzed. Finally, the team specified the attributes used to find the similarities and differences between customer clusters.

The results of the data mining model were stored in the source OLAP cube that the team used to create the mining model. This OLAP cube provides end users with a fast, multidimensional view of the "mined" customer sales data. To allow users to query data stored in the OLAP cube, Microsoft Excel was selected as the end user data access tool. Excel already was a familiar tool for business users; however, users were only familiar with static spreadsheets. To help users understand how to interact with the customer sales data, the data warehouse team created basic Excel templates that businesspeople could use to query the data in the OLAP cube. In addition, the team performed an internal training session to teach business users how to use the interactive analysis features of OLAP using Excel.

Another specific business scenario that the marketing department wanted to understand was the characteristics describing customers in each level of the DiscoPlus program based on accumulated points. For this project, the data warehouse team decided to create a data mining model with a **decision tree**, which was used to break data into groups. This is often the simplest model for nontechnical users to understand because the results found by the decision tree are displayed visually and can be interactively explored.

A decision tree uses a statistical algorithm to split the set of data being mined into branches of a tree. The first split is selected by testing the value of each field in the data, such as age or gender, and finding the rule that separates the data into two partitions. Each partition contains data that is most similar with data in its own partition while most diverse from data in the other partition. For example, an initial split may find that homeowners and renters form the best separation of customers. After the initial split, the decision tree algorithm continues by examining the remaining fields to find the best split of these two partitions so that there are now four partitions. To continue with the example, the homeowner's branch may split between married and single homeowners, while the renter's branch may split between customers under 40 and customers over 40. This process continues until no further splits can be found. When interpreting a tree, the result of the first split is most significant and most reliable, while subsequent splits become increasingly less accurate since the set of data within a partition becomes smaller at each split.

To create the decision tree for the marketing department, the OLAP cube containing DiscoPlus data could again be used to build the data mining model. The results of the data mining model can be viewed in Analysis Services, which allows the user to interactively explore each branch of the decision tree. The results of this decision tree showed that age, geographical location, and marital status were, respectively, the top three fields that characterized the DiscoPlus point level attained by each customer. For example, an analysis of customers in the platinum level, which is the highest point level of the program, showed that the greatest percentage of these customers was between 42 years old and 48 years old.

Solution Benefits

Within one month of the original start date, the first implementation of the BI solution was complete, and the marketing department now had fast and easy access to consistent customer sales information thanks to the advanced analytical techniques made possible with data mining technology. By applying the correct data mining technique to the business problem, Disco has been able to take action to improve sales and customer relations. With segmentation and clustering, a profile has been built for specific groups of customers, which allows Disco to send the right message to the right audience. Similarly, decision trees provide the type of information that allows Disco to focus on providing the types of quality products and services desired by specific age groups and thus ensure customer loyalty for years to come.

The marketing department has since used data mining to understand how promotional campaigns affect the product choices that customers make. For example, when Disco started selling a new brand of milk, a new data mining project was launched to characterize the buying habits of the customer base. Before the promotion, customers were segmented into groups: those who bought a specific brand of milk and those who never bought milk. After the promotion was run, data mining was used to compare the precampaign groups with the postcampaign groups of customers who switched to the new milk, customers who bought more milk, customers who stopped buying milk, and customers who switched to a different brand. With the insights gained from this analysis, marketing dollars for future campaigns can be spent more efficiently by targeting customers who will respond, leading to higher product sales.

The marketing department at Disco now better understands customer behavior and is able to design marketing campaigns that are more appropriate to each profile. Customers with similar profiles receive information only about products and services that are of interest to them. As a result of these new campaigns, Disco has not only delivered on its promise of quality customer service but has also benefited from a fast return on its investment. "In some cases, one hundred percent return," said Diaz.

In addition to the insights provided by data mining, business users in the pricing, marketing, accounting, and merchandising departments at each of the five headquarter offices across Argentina now have direct access to the data warehouse to retrieve answers to their questions without having to rely on IT to deliver information. Since the sales data is already stored in an OLAP cube in preparation for data mining, users can quickly access information about sales, margins, cost, revenue, and stock levels and can develop their own reports to analyze this information by store, department, manager, supplier, product, sales channel, and category management classifications.

Even better, the data warehouse contains information about the previous day's sales, which is a marked improvement from weekly sales data. Decision makers are now able to respond quickly to trends as they become apparent. Ocaranza noted that the data warehouse project has provided "powerful tools, speed, and independence for our users to make decisions."

Project Challenges

Successfully implementing the BI solution required the data warehouse team to address a few project challenges. One of the challenges encountered by the data warehouse team was that the process required users to be educated in using the data warehouse. Since the users' experience had been limited to data provided in spreadsheets, the concept of interactive exploration of data was very foreign to them at first. The data warehouse team presented seminars to explain what a data warehouse allows the users to accomplish and what the benefits of the data warehouse would mean for them. The Excel templates created by the team enabled users to start simply and develop their skills for more advanced interaction with OLAP data. These efforts have proven quite successful. Diaz commented: "Our users are eager for more information from the data warehouse system."

The data warehouse team faced a bigger challenge with data quality. The results of data mining can be dramatically affected by data of poor quality, data that is incomplete, or data with too few records to be mined; thus data preparation often represents the longest and most complex phase of a data mining project. Because the DiscoPlus program had been implemented several years ago, the way in which data was gathered and cleansed had changed many times since its inception. As a result, there were issues with data accuracy that could be resolved only through reengineering the data extraction and transformation processes. However, this extra effort to adequately collect and prepare the data has resulted in a data warehouse that can support many successful data mining projects to come.

Summary

Disco has made possible faster and better decision making through its successful deployment of innovative BI technology. In effect, the company has added value to information by expanding its use through the application of data mining techniques and enabling its employees to achieve a greater understanding of the customer base.

The data warehouse team has plans to leverage Disco's BI investment by expanding its capabilities. Mining models will be developed to build predictive models to detect the fraudulent use of credit cards, which will ultimately reduce corporate losses. Also planned is the extension of the data warehouse into other areas of the organization, such as procurement, logistics, receivables, and payables.

Step by step, Disco is providing its employees with access to faster, reliable, and more analytical information. Each employee, empowered through greater knowledge and deeper insights obtained with business intelligence, can contribute to the creation of a positive customer experience and thus to the ongoing success of the company.

Managing Seasonal Variability—Cascade Designs

We design products with superior engineering and manufacture them here in North America to unsurpassed quality. When manufacturing advanced products like ours, there is no way you can maintain high efficiency and high quality if you lay off your workforce with each slow season—and providing some stability for your people is just the right thing to do. To be successful with this approach, in a highly seasonal business like ours, demands superior operational efficiency and excellent forecasting.

—Lee Fromson, Chief Operating Officer, Cascade Designs

When you visit the headquarters of Cascade Designs in the Sodo district of Seattle, you can't help but notice the dramatic photos of intrepid adventurers standing atop some of the world's highest mountains. Given that the company is a privately held manufacturer of outdoor lifestyle products, with annual sales in excess of $50 million, this is hardly surprising. But what is unusual about the photos at Cascade Designs is that many of the people pictured are the same people who work there. "Up, down, and across the organizational chart, this company has people who can achieve great things under the harshest conditions—and regularly," says Lee Fromson, Chief Operating Officer (COO). "That creates a self-confidence and self-discipline that people bring back to the office. Nature has a way of teaching you how to prioritize and focus on what is really important right now." The ability to prioritize and focus was exactly what was needed when Cascade Designs decided to implement a new JD Edwards **enterprise resource planning (ERP) system**. This initiative was largely motivated by the desire to improve efficiency and scalability and also provide substantial benefits in corporate-wide business intelligence.

Case study information collected through interviews conducted by Aspirity, LLC, of Bellevue, Washington.

Company Background

The company was founded in 1972, when Jim Lea, a former Boeing engineering manager with a passion for the outdoors, used his knowledge of space-age technology to invent a lightweight, self-inflating sleeping pad for backpackers. The first product, the Therm-a-Rest pad, was a smashing success and quickly became an essential accessory for every outdoor enthusiast; as a result, Cascade Designs won the outdoor industry's *SNEWS (Sporting Goods News Trade Magazine)* award for "best small company with a limited product line" 16 straight years. Following this initial success, the company expanded not only its line of sleeping pads but also introduced water filters, hydration systems, cooking stoves, and other equipment for the active outdoors person.

You will not find any fashion products at Cascade Designs—products that are all the rage one year but unwanted the next. However, you will find the kind of products you are glad to own 10 years after you bought them, especially when you are on the side of a mountain and depending on them to perform. This commitment to creating the highest quality in outdoor products goes well beyond the engineers; every manager is expected to spend a considerable amount of time in the wilderness field-testing products—both the company's own products and those from competitors.

The business model at Cascade Designs is that of a classic manufacturing company. Rather than selling directly to retail consumers, the company sells its products to over 1000 wholesale distributors and retail stores—its retail "channels." More than half of the company's sales are outside the United States.

The company's strategy is to design products with superior engineering and to manufacture them in North America to unsurpassed quality. This approach implies several operational challenges, including the relatively high cost of manufacturing in North America, the extreme seasonality of the outdoor sporting goods business, and the logistical challenges of shipping product all over the world. According to Lee Fromson,

> For the advanced products that we manufacture, there is no way you can maintain high efficiency and high quality if you lay off your workforce with each slow season—and providing some stability for your people is just the right thing to do. Clearly to be successful in this approach, we need superior operational efficiency and excellent forecasting.

Business Requirements

After several years of growth and a couple of mergers, Cascade Designs' computer systems consisted of a diverse collection of loosely integrated, stand-alone applications. The numerous integrating pieces were all developed and supported internally by a few key people. This was not a good use of their time and somewhat risky; remember, these are the same people who spend their weekends climbing mountains. In addition, the complexity of the system was limiting the efficiency and growth of the company. People were growing increasingly frustrated, often ending up with insufficient or inappropriate raw materials, having too much or too little finished product, or having the wrong product in the wrong location.

These people convinced the COO of the severity of the problem, and he agreed to sponsor a project to find solutions and take corrective action. According to Lee Fromson,

> Our systems were becoming a liability, preventing us from executing and limiting our future options. Initially we thought we could solve the problems by developing a new reporting system, but the more we looked at everything, the more we realized that we had to completely replace our current operational systems and not merely build a BI system downstream of our existing systems. We had too many problems in the disconnected source systems; we needed a tightly integrated operational system.

Eventually Cascade Designs decided to implement a top-end ERP application package that would support not only current needs but also future growth of up to 30 times greater than the company's current size. Having systems capable of supporting that scale of growth—and particularly growth by acquisition—was important to the overall strategy of the company.

While implementation of an ERP application would help improve efficiency, address concerns of maintainability, and provide a platform for future growth, it was clear that it would also create problems. According to Fromson,

> While we knew there would be operational reporting improvements, we were aware that we would also be creating a big reporting problem. None of the ERP packages we looked at provided an adequate

ad hoc reporting solution. They all created this monstrous pile of data that was truly overwhelming. Immediately on implementing the new ERP system, all legacy reporting systems would be obsolete, and with the cost of the high-end ERP system, we would have little money left to invest.

For a company with a strategy that depends on excellent forecasting and reporting, this problem was a serious concern.

Fromson continued:

We have a distinctly bipolar approach to planning. We think any five-year plan is not worth the paper it is printed on. Life is too chaotic to waste time planning five years out. Instead, for the long term, we strive for a broad understanding of our opportunities, issues, and strategies. We discuss these often and widely, but this is not a plan. For the short term—the next season—we have a completely different approach. We forecast at our lowest level of details (each product item for each retail outlet), and we review it frequently. Now that's a plan we can use to manage inventory and production levels.

In addition to its internal information sources, Cascade Designs needed to make use of many external sources to obtain market intelligence, such as channel partners, external market share resources, and advisory panels who discuss consumer interests and trends.

A key asset for making accurate forecasting possible is a unique preseason order program (POP) that was developed some years ago by John Burroughs, President of Cascade Designs and one of the company founders. This tool is basically a sales automation and forecasting tool, where sales representatives enter preseason orders at a detailed level. The information is then transferred to central operational systems by using **electronic data interchange (EDI)**. It has been so effective that it is now licensed by other manufacturers to forecast sales for their products. This tool provides a competitive advantage, and replacing it with a commercial package is not in the near-term plan. The POP forecast needs to be integrated with the actual orders that come from the ERP.

A similar problem existed with regard to departmental budgets. These budgets are built in and maintained using a software package called Pillar from Hyperion Solutions. Performing variance analysis requires comparing the budget data from Pillar to actual data from the ERP.

The Solution

Choosing the ERP software vendor was a key decision. On one hand, Cascade Designs did not like the high cost and rigidity of some large enterprise solutions; on the other hand, the company was concerned about the scalability and long-term viability of some smaller vendors. JD Edwards ERP system was eventually selected, with Microsoft SQL Server as the relational database platform. This system serves as the ultimate system of record for products, customers, and business units. According to Fromson,

> This was a huge initiative for us. We were successful because the entire management team was involved in making decisions. Philosophically, we place responsibility for systems in the functional areas, not IT; IT is in a supporting role only. Once we made the decision to do it, we knew we had to finish as quickly as possible. It's much too painful to stretch out a major change like this; it consumes so much time from all managers and affects so many plans that it can freeze the entire company if you don't put the implementation behind you in a hurry. What if something really important happens in your markets and all your managers are tied up working on the system implementation?

After implementing the operational systems, Cascade Designs added OLAP data marts for analysis using Microsoft SQL Server 2000 Analysis Services with Microsoft Excel as the client access tool. Figure 8.1 illustrates the architecture. Information is collected from the ERP system and other source systems using Microsoft SQL Server 2000 Data Transformation Services (DTS) and placed in a staging database. The OLAP data marts are created using DTS as well.

According to Barry Paxman, Cascade's IT Manager

> Frankly, we chose these technologies because they were mostly free for us. We had already licensed the SQL Server infrastructure to support the JD Edwards ERP system, and our users already had Excel and pretty much love it. If this approach had not met our needs, we would have looked at alternatives, but it worked out pretty well. The IT department brings the data together from all the source systems and builds cubes for the users to browse using Excel.

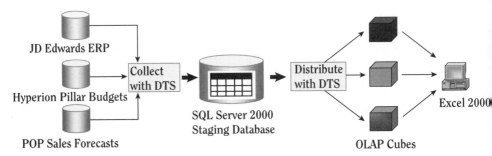

Figure 8-1. *System architecture*

The OLAP tool is primarily for sales analysis, with cubes for inventory, orders, and comparisons between actual and plan. The plan data is by customer by product by month—typically within a one-year planning horizon. Dimensions include product, plant, time, geography, channel, sales representative, incentive program, customer segment, and others. In addition to the JD Edwards ERP system, the OLAP cubes also include data from other sources. This allows managers to compare the plan to actual orders at different levels of summarization, giving both a sanity check to the plan and a mechanism for identifying problem areas.

Solution Benefits

The new, centralized JD Edwards ERP system has already resulted in substantial cost savings that have provided payback for the investment. The new system keeps better track of inventories by maintaining tight control of the cycle count process. As a result, Cascade's external auditors have given a green light to discontinue the practice of a semiannual shutdown of the factory to perform complete physical inventories—a task that required four days to complete. The estimated value of this benefit alone is over $70,000 per year.

Other benefits were realized when Cascade Designs recently acquired a company approximately half its size. The ERP system made it possible to combine the operations of both companies in only three months by using only internal resources. The fast integration not only allowed Cascade Designs to quickly get orders to customers but also enabled the company to quickly cut in half the combined accounting staff of the two companies. This was clear evidence that the strategic objective of being able to support growth by acquisition was being met.

The new system has also proven valuable for making better product decisions. For example, previous cost models indicated that manufacturing carabiners for rock climbers was a profitable business. The new system allowed a more accurate calculation of total product cost, including fixed costs and indirect engineering costs, which indicated that the product cost more to manufacture than key customers were willing to pay. The company has dropped the product to focus on more profitable products.

Inventory management and procurement have improved. For example, the improvement of raw material inventory tracking has reduced shortages and allowed more aggressive management of these inventories. Also, when the cost of a particular raw material spiked much higher than expected, this was identified quickly, and a cost-saving alternative was rapidly found.

The OLAP portion has also worked very well. It took less than two weeks to implement the first cube, a fraction of the operational systems. The cost was also very modest because additional software licenses were not required. Because of OLAP, Cascade Designs was able to move from the "monstrous pile of data" to easy access to all customers and products. In addition to meeting the requirements of comparing budgets and forecasts against actual orders and performing variance analysis, individual departments can now analyze their own data without having to ask IT to create special reports. Rather than taking days or even weeks to just get the data, data is now retrieved fast enough to make real-time decisions.

Now that the company can roll up the entire mix of products, terms, conditions, write-offs, and discounts, Cascade Designs can see the big picture for each customer. It can now analyze profitability by customer and differentiate those who contribute substantial profits from those who contribute marginal profits. By analyzing customers in this way, the company discovered a number of surprises, such as customers who consistently received extensive attention but contributed little to the bottom line, and others who were frustrating to work with, perhaps demanding special conditions or allowances, but who turned out to be some of the most profitable customers.

Lessons Learned

According to Fromson,

> We were ahead of the curve in our choice of SQL Server and the JD Edwards ERP system as the platform. The early releases were

frustrating to work with. The project was definitely more painful than anticipated because while senior managers were heavily involved in the systems implementation, the rest of the business suffered—a major hidden cost. But platform choice and extensive involvement of management, while very painful, are not decisions I would want to go back and change. They were investments and are paying off. Looking back, the thing I would change would be getting more training up front to our people. We were in such a rush to get the system running that we did not spend enough time on training. As a consequence, users took more time to learn the new tools and made some mistakes that could have been prevented. That was a waste. With regard to the OLAP implementation—it was so easy, inexpensive, and effective—we should have been using it sooner, even before the ERP system.

Future Plans

Some parts of the business, such as foreign operations, are not yet included in the integrated system. In addition, the company sees more opportunities down the road, for example, managing the supply chain and automating communication with vendors and customers. New system enhancements, however, will need to wait at least for a little while, as managers catch their breath, reap the benefits of the current investment, and focus on other opportunities. For example, when Cascade Designs discovered that medical professionals were recommending its outdoor mattress products to patients as back rests and for other therapeutic purposes, the company realized that it had an entirely new set of potential customers.

Summary

To operate a competitive manufacturing business in the United States, where many costs are higher than in other countries, efficiency is critical. Maintaining a stable workforce in a highly seasonal industry requires careful attention to production scheduling and inventory management. Combining these requirements demands tight control and excellent information. The new systems provide many improvements in both of these areas.

A Business Intelligence Roadmap

In Part I you discovered what business intelligence is and how it can help you make better decisions faster. In Part II you learned how other companies have benefited from it. In Part III you will learn how to apply these lessons in business intelligence to your own organization. To guide your BI initiatives, Part III describes how you can develop a BI roadmap that identifies what your organization wants to achieve with business intelligence and how it will get there.

Chapter 9, "Identifying BI Opportunities," describes the first goal of the BI roadmap—identifying what you want to achieve with business intelligence. The chapter provides practical advice for helping you jump-start your BI initiatives, including techniques for finding opportunities to improve the quality of departmental, business unit, and company-wide decision making; a process for brainstorming the types of information that can help you fulfill these opportunities; and guidelines for ranking the importance and difficulty of each potential opportunity area. The most prominent BI opportunities and the information requirements that support them become the basis for what you want to achieve with business intelligence.

Chapter 10, "Implementing a BI Solution," describes the second goal of the BI roadmap—how to create a BI solution to help you take advantage of the BI opportunities defined in Chapter 9. The chapter serves as an implementation guide designed especially for business decision makers. The guide is divided into two parts: (1) an implementation strategy for successfully building a BI solution and (2) practical advice for making the fundamental decisions involved with creating a BI solution. These decisions include assembling an implementation team, choosing the appropriate technology and tools, making design decisions about dimensions and measures, and making judgment calls about the source data.

Identifying BI Opportunities

The first task in starting a BI initiative—and the first goal of the BI roadmap—is identifying what you want to achieve with business intelligence. In practical terms this means looking for opportunities in your organization where business intelligence can improve the quality of day-to-day decision making. An organization will likely have many of these opportunities, both within and across various functional areas and business units. With limited time and money in the organization, however, the key is deciding which opportunities offer the most value.

The purpose of this chapter is to describe an easy-to-use process for brainstorming and evaluating specific BI opportunity areas in an organization. This process is divided into three primary steps:

- *Doing your homework* requires consideration of where business intelligence can be applied in an organization (for example, business units or functional areas), who is to benefit (for example, executives, analysts, and managers), and what types of information are needed (for example, dimensions and measures).

- *Sharing and collecting ideas* involves gathering people together to brainstorm and share their ideas and experiences about which business processes can benefit from business intelligence and what information can help them improve these processes.

- *Evaluating alternatives* uses standard criteria to assess the ideas collected during brainstorming efforts and identify those BI opportunities that offer the greatest benefits.

Doing Your Homework

Doing your homework is based on an old news reporter adage: "Just tell me who, what, where, why, when, and how." We bend this adage somewhat by trimming down the number of "w" questions and reorganizing the order.

The how question—"How to implement business intelligence"—is addressed in Chapter 10, "Implementing a BI Solution." The following three questions represent the most significant considerations for identifying BI opportunities:

- *Where* will the BI application be used in the organization?

- *Who* are the users, both within organizational units and at higher levels?

- *What* information is needed—specifically, what measures and dimensions?

Where Will Business Intelligence Be Used?

Answering the question "Where will business intelligence be used?" requires investigating which areas of the organization can benefit from business intelligence. While every organization is set up differently, a great place to begin the investigation is by examining the critical processes of the organization's **functional areas** and **business units**. We define the term *business unit* as an organizational structure in which a coherent set of functional activities rolls up into one line of business. For example, Hewlett Packard Corporation is an *enterprise,* with storage, printing and imaging, and servers and network business units. Large conglomerates, for example, General Electric Corporation, typically have hundreds of business units. For some companies such as CompUSA, where business activities are homogeneous across the corporation, the terms *enterprise* and *business unit* occur at the same top level. We define the term *functional area* as a department of a business unit that is focused on a specific function—finance, marketing, sales, human resources, and so forth.

Whether you are investigating a functional area or business unit, the questions that need to be considered are pretty straightforward:

- What is working vs. what is broken?

- Where are you spending too much money for the apparent return?

- What processes are taking too much time?

- Where do you think you are missing opportunities?

- Where are you making bad decisions?

- Where are you making good decisions?

A review of critical functional areas and processes will quickly uncover many opportunities for consideration. Unlike traditional financial analysis, BI techniques are universally applicable to any area of business, and broken departmental processes can often be significantly improved or better managed with the faster and better information that business intelligence delivers.

The case studies in Part II of this book illustrated the value of using business intelligence to improve the core processes of various functional areas. At CompUSA the results of BI efforts were measurable store-level improvements in employee selling performance, loss prevention, and warranty data collection. The major savings and efficiencies at Audi AG were achieved in assembly line production because of better scheduling and managing of the product mix. Revenues at Disco S.A. were improved through the precise tuning of product offerings to customer segments. These examples of process improvements in functional areas are all extremely important to running the company on a day-to-day basis and making money.

Applying business intelligence to functional areas is an excellent place to begin your practice of business intelligence. The requirements for functional areas are generally easier to define, and the benefits are easier to conceptualize and measure than more aggressive BI endeavors that cross several functional areas. A functional BI application can also be relatively easier to implement because source data often comes from only one or a few OLTP systems as opposed to cross-functional or business-unit level applications that typically combine data from multiple sources. Functional area BI applications also tend to be more tactical in nature, oriented to the management of specific operations or employee behavior, rather than strategic and foundational to the basic directions of the company. For all these reasons, functional applications are typically the first baby steps of applied business intelligence.

A step up from functional or departmental BI applications are cross-functional and business-unit applications. These applications tend to be more strategic and oriented to high-level planning rather than the tuning of operational details. Consider the following examples of cross-functional and business-unit applications.

- Product and product line contribution analysis: In this application of business intelligence, variable costs are collected from all functional areas of the business, not just variable manufacturing costs, and then assigned or allocated to specific products or product lines. The potential payoffs are better understanding of alternative pricing strategies, pruning of unprofitable products or product lines, and new bundling of product offerings.

- Customer profitability analysis: In this application, revenues and costs are collected and then allocated to specific customers and customer groupings. The potential payoffs are customer (or customer group) pricing or discount structures, customer product differentiation, customer pruning, and channel economic analysis.

Because these applications are used by staff and managers from multiple departments, they are more difficult to define and obtain agreement on. Because they typically involve data from multiple functional areas (that is, multiple OLTP systems), they tend to be more difficult to build. Because the payoff is measured by better decisions rather than operational performance improvements, it is more difficult to identify the benefits when evaluating the opportunity and measure the results when the implementation is complete. Cross-functional and business-unit applications are essentially about decision making and strategic issues that are paramount to protecting and enhancing competitive advantage; they have potential for the greatest payoff and are more advanced forms of business intelligence.

While corporate strategies and goals are implemented from the top down, from the enterprise level of an organization to individual business units, business intelligence is typically implemented as a bottom-up process, with performance metrics originating from the business-unit level. Remember our discussion of key performance indicators (KPIs) in Chapter 1? Except in the most homogeneous of large corporations, enterprise-level business intelligence is usually only reporting KPIs from business units rather than drilling down through hierarchies to reach organizational details. These business unit KPIs tend to vary from unit to unit. For example, the consulting services business unit of a software manufacturer will examine KPIs such as staff utilization rates, while its retail business unit will analyze KPIs such as the number of customers and average selling price.

While these KPIs reflect the unique functions of each business unit, at an enterprise level it is important to compare performance among multiple business units. To do this, a company needs to have some top-down metrics that are driven by corporate management. These metrics are most likely standard financial indicators, such as revenue, margins, and costs.

Who Will Use the Application?

While focusing on critical processes in functional and cross-functional areas of the business is of primary importance when identifying BI opportunities, understanding who will use the application is another important factor that must be considered. More specifically, you need to think through the information and analysis needs of the different roles and levels in the organization—operators, supervisors, managers, senior managers, and analysts.

The rule of thumb is fairly simple: the lower the job classification of the target user, the more likely the need for detailed data that is operational in nature and particular to a specific functional area; the higher the job classification, the more likely the need for summarized data that supports the analysis of trends and patterns within and across functional areas.

Consider the following example of a telephone call center. Call center operators typically work with transaction-level information, including customer names and addresses, product numbers and descriptions, and so forth; this information is routinely provided by the company's OLTP system. The need may also be the same for the first-line supervisors whose roles are to help operators with a difficult or troubling problem. Now let's consider the customer support manager who oversees the operation. While this manager occasionally needs ground zero transaction detail, he or she more likely uses multidimensional and hierarchical information that describes operational performance, such as average response time to calls and customer satisfaction by shift, by department, by hour of day, and by support agent.

This example illustrates that the people who use a specific BI application are important considerations while sorting through BI opportunities and priorities within a functional area. BI systems have also made possible a new phenomenon—the easy access to operational information by analysts, senior managers, and executives *outside* the functional department. Traditional operations reporting up the company hierarchy have been slow, limited in scope, and paper based and therefore not of great interest or limited in usefulness to higher management. With business intelligence—fast, broad in scope, and not paper based—senior managers can quickly look into day-to-day operations, check out trends, follow up on hunches, and act quickly. Business intelligence empowers higher levels of management in new ways not previously possible—assuming company politics can be aligned, of course, which is no trivial task.

The Frank Russell Company in Chapter 5 provides an excellent example of empowering managers with valuable information. While its Picasso solution certainly improved operational performance within the various fund management groups, it also gave higher level managers broader and more timely information about overall assets under management, selling trends, and fund performance. This same benefit—more senior access to information—continued with the implementation of Einstein. For CompUSA in Chapter 6, a relatively homogeneous company in its business-unit organization, the BI system was designed to provide senior management with faster, more focused operational reporting and improved visibility at the store and district level.

As you determine who will use your BI application, try to think how your application can service the need of different users. What may first look like a moderately interesting opportunity within a functional area could prove to be very interesting and gain strong political support if the BI designs incorporate the interests of staff or senior managers higher up or outside the functional area.

What Information Do You Need?

When looking for BI opportunities in an organization, defining what information offers the most value to that organization is an absolute and fundamental requirement. Put simply, you need to connect the dots between the decisions or processes you want to effect, the measures on which you want to focus (for example, sales amount, number of customers, and profit margin), the dimensions you need for analysis (for example, time, product, and customer), and the raw data you have available (or that must be created) from multiple OLTP systems and other data sources.

Certainly, your mental model of how the business works is essential to establishing information requirements. Mostly, though, you need to work hard and steadily through the details and ask lots of questions. The following is a three-step guide that can help you consider the types of information you need.

Define the Measures

Most companies have a standard set of metrics and financial indicators for keeping track of the business and measuring a company's performance. Collectively these are known as measures. Historically, standard measures have been predominantly financial and single dimensional in nature. The measures for a business in today's world should focus on the critical success factors for each functional area, including additional parameters for measuring the broader strategies, goals, and objectives of the company as a whole. Ultimately, there must be a strong linkage between departmental performance indicators and top-level metrics for gauging the effectiveness of the company strategy and achieving goals and objectives.

A good way to start defining the measures for functional areas is by determining what metrics describe the performance of the base activities and the most important processes of a department. Metrics can be divided into two general categories: **base measures** and **calculated measures**. Base measures are measures that are captured at the transaction level. For example, unit sales data and amount sales data are both important base measures captured on a sales transaction. Average price, on the other hand, is not a base measure. Average price is a calculated measure that is computed by dividing the amount sales by unit sales for any aggregation of sales orders. Headcount is another example of a base measure. When amount sales is divided by headcount, the calculated measure sales per head—an important productivity metric—is created. Thinking through calculated measures that can be derived from base measures is a great method for identifying rich and easily obtained department performance indicators.

The most relevant measures are driven by the functional area and processes for which the BI application is being developed—the *where* consideration discussed earlier in this chapter. For example, sales-related measures (unit sales, amount sales, count of orders, backlog, and so forth) are relevant for the sales organization; production measures (assembly units, hours, inventory, and so forth) are relevant for the production department; employee measures (turnover, tenure, employee satisfaction, absenteeism, and so forth) are relevant for the human resources department. These should be obvious connections.

Less obvious is the impact of users—the *who* consideration discussed earlier. Here are two useful but not absolute rules of thumb:

- The lower the organizational level of a user, the greater the interest in the absolute values of a particular measure within a specific time period, especially compared to a benchmark or other measure of expected performance. For example, for a given day or week, what is the average minutes per call for customer support operators vs. a set standard? Lower levels of BI users focus mostly on short-term, correctable performance.

- The higher the organizational level of a user, especially one who is *outside the functional department,* the greater the focus on trends of measures over time. For example, are the average minutes per call going up or down during the last week or month? Trends are typically more important than absolutes.

Define the Dimensions

First measures; then dimensions. Once you understand the important measures for an application, you can then define the dimensions in which the measures can be described. (Recall from Chapter 2 that dimensions are defined as category-consistent views that provide context to measures.)

To understand how dimensions interact with measures, let's walk through a simple example: assume you want to analyze gross margins by product by region by quarter for the year 2001. The key word is *by;* it indicates a dimension reference. The breakdown of this analysis into dimensions and measures is as follows:

- The base measures are amount sales, unit sales, and unit cost. The calculated measures are cost (unit sales multiplied by unit cost) and gross margin (amount sales minus cost).

- The dimensions are time (quarters 1 through 4), products (A through C), and regions (1 through 3).

This example is simple and illustrates several precepts for defining the information that you need for a BI application:

- Decide on the measures and how they interrelate and are calculated *before* defining dimensions.

- Consider how you want to analyze measures over time. In almost all BI applications, you will find a time dimension. Time parameters are driven by the time horizon in which the BI analysis needs to be performed.

- While specifying dimensions, start thinking generally about where the data will come from or recognize early on the need to construct new ones from scratch if the dimension need is important enough.

- Instead of thinking of each of dimension singly, consider how multiple dimensions can describe a particular measure. Recall from the fruit seller example in Chapter 2 that analysis across multiple dimensions simultaneously makes the data useful for analysis.

Common Dimensions

To help define information requirements, here is a list of common dimensions found in typical BI applications across different functional areas:

- *Sales and Marketing*—products, customers, demographics (age group, gender), sales channel, geography, promotions, campaigns, sales force, order status, sales type, time

- *Human Resources*—organizational chart, employees, time, business unit, department

- *Operations*—shift, time, assembly line, product, manufacturer, warehouse, suppliers

- *Finance*—currency, account, scenario, time, business unit, department

---

Define the Level of Detail

For each combination of dimensions and measures, decide how much detail is desired; that is, what is the lowest level of information for each dimension that must be available across different user groups? Defining the lowest level is an important decision because all summarized data can be easily derived from the lowest level of detail.

Business requirements should drive the decisions about level of detail, yet be tempered by common sense. When you consider how much detail is required, consider the relative implications of summarized vs. detailed data. Summarized or high-level data tends to minimize the number of data points that you have to analyze, but it does not allow you to see trends at lower levels of detail. On the other hand, less summarized or low-level data means that you will need to analyze more data points to identify trends.

Consider the following example: a point-of-sale system contains up-to-the-minute sales information by customer, store, and product. At a rate of 10 sales per minute for 10 hours per day for 365 days a year, nearly 2.2 million data points are collected. If you view sales data summarized by month, you will not be able to see weekly, daily, and hourly trends. On the other hand, if you analyze data at its lowest level of detail—minute-by-minute—you will not be able to identify meaningful patterns. Rather, in this case, meaningful patterns begin to appear at the hour level.

Realistically, you will need some combination of both summarized and detailed views of the data to meet the analysis needs of all business users. The key is to strike a balance. The technique to finding this balance is deciding on a reasonable level of detail for the lowest level of data required across all users and then using the BI system to create hierarchical summaries from the detail. For detailed data, you also have the option to apply more advanced analytical techniques, for example, data mining, that thrive on crunching through large amounts of detailed data to find trends that are invisible to the human eye. After deciding on the level of detail, your IT organization can help evaluate the feasibility of accessing the data.

Sharing and Collecting Ideas

In the previous section we described considerations to help you identify BI opportunities in your organization. Based on these considerations, the objective of this section is to outline a step-by-step process for sharing and collecting ideas from other people in your organization. The process has five steps:

1. Arrange a brainstorming session.

2. Define the brainstorming team.

3. Ask business questions.

4. Identify information requirements.

5. Organize information requirements.

Arrange a Brainstorming Session

A brainstorming session is an opportunity to gather a group of people together to discuss which business processes can benefit from business intelligence and what types of information can help them improve these processes. The goals of the brainstorming session are to develop a list of business questions and create a definition of the information that will provide the perspective to answer those questions—specifically, the important measures and dimensions. In reality this may take the form of one or more brainstorming sessions.

To facilitate each brainstorming session, we recommend using large sticky notes to document the brainstorming session. Sticky notes provide a quick, visual snapshot of group discussions and can be placed on the wall of an office or conference room to remind participants of what was said and document key information for later write-up. Because sticky notes are easy to move around, they also help participants identify and keep track of relationships among various information requirements.

Define the Brainstorming Team

The topic of a brainstorming session typically drives who attends. For exploring opportunities in a specific functional area, invite users, analysts, and managers from that functional area to the session. Be sure to include the experts for the information-driven processes of the department or departments in the functional area. Brainstorming discussions will explore how the process currently works and where the information is coming from. The ready availability of one or more experts to describe current processes and data sources will move the brainstorming session forward. For exploring cross-functional opportunities, invite participants from the affected areas. Cross-functional opportunities frequently involve financial considerations. When that is the case, make sure that you involve a financial analyst who understands accounting and cost-system sources.

Brainstorming sessions should definitely be business driven. Therefore, involving the IT organization at this early stage may not be necessary. An IT representative can offer perspective, but do not discourage free-form discussion by worrying too soon about technical considerations, such as the availability of certain data or how and when the data extraction process might work. The IT department should be involved at later stages once hard BI design questions are being proposed.

Brainstorming works best when one person skilled at the process facilitates the session, including writing ideas on the sticky notes.

Ask Business Questions

The second step is asking questions without worrying about the answers. Our experience is that letting users articulate the typical questions asked in the day-to-day running of the business elicits rich information about measures and dimensions. Here are examples of the kinds of questions you may hear:

- Which product lines are generating the most margin in Florida?
- Why do we get more support calls from the West Coast than other regions?
- Who are the top sales representatives in the United States?
- When was the last time we saw this surprising pattern in product X sales?
- Why are sales so low in France this month?

"Why" questions are often the most interesting. They typically translate into many "what?" subquestions. For example, the question, "Why are sales so low in France?" could lead to the following questions:

- What is the forecast for sales in France?
- What were the sales in France last month? In the same month a year ago?
- What products are the biggest sellers in France?

The phrasing of questions provides important clues about measures and dimensions. To document the clues, do the following for each of the most important questions:

1. Write the question at the top of a sticky note. Leave room on the sticky note for information that will come later. Use only one sticky note per question.

2. Number the sticky notes sequentially and place them on the office or conference room wall. Post questions from the same functional area adjacent to each other.

3. If the brainstorming session is for cross-functional opportunities, for example, customer profitability analysis, use different-colored sticky notes for each department to capture its key questions or tag the sticky notes with the department name.

Figure 9-1 presents what a set of sticky notes might look like with questions posted.

Figure 9-1. *Brainstorming questions on sticky notes*

Identify Information Requirements

Once a meaningful sample of questions is documented, these can be translated into specifications for measures and dimensions—the objective of the exercise. The brainstorming group must think through what information is needed to answer the questions.

You can identify information requirements in any of three ways: by discussing the requirements within the group, by looking at current reports, or by using a sticky note or whiteboard to sketch sample reports with rows and headers that identify the information. Whatever the method, the objective is to state the measure or measures underlying each question and then identify the relevant dimensions for answering the question. Write the measures under the question on the sticky note and then write the dimensions below, connecting each with the word *by*. In addition, for each dimension add in parentheses the lowest level of detail likely required for answering the questions within the dimension area; that is, estimate the likely lowest level for drilling down.

Figure 9-2 presents the three questions on sticky notes that we asked earlier with a mapping of measures, dimensions, and lowest level of detail just described. Note that we have added additional measures that are implied but not obviously stated in the question. For example, for the product line in Florida question (#1), to analyze margin you need revenue and cost information. For the top sales representative question (#3), the measure was not explicitly stated in the question; therefore, several measures related to sales, orders, and commissions are suggested. Note also that all questions by default get a time dimension designation that the group decides on. The lowest level time horizon reflects the level at which meaningful trends occur.

Notice that several dimensions are included on the support call sticky note question (#2). The geography dimension is obvious because geography is referenced in the question. After discussion, however, the brainstorming group added customer and product, noting that this information was captured at the beginning of each call and that customer and product types

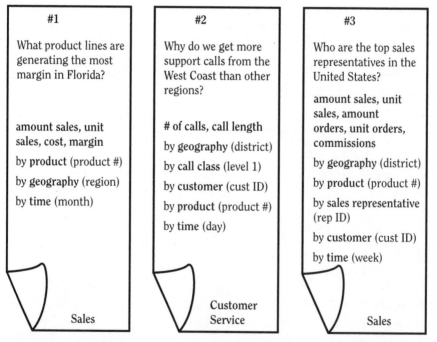

Figure 9-2. *Brainstorming questions with supporting measures and dimensions*

were very likely drivers of call pattern anomalies such as the one asked in the question.

Organize the Information Requirements

In the final step of the brainstorming process, organize the sticky note information by logging the measures and dimension information into a special table called a **BI blueprint**. In the columns of the blueprint, document dimension names. In the rows fill in the sticky note number references and measures. At each intersection of dimension and measure, post the lowest level of detail for that dimension. If a dimension does not apply to a measure, enter *NA* (not applicable) in the cell.

Table 9-1 is a sample BI blueprint that organizes the information from the example sticky notes presented in Figure 9-2.

Table 9-1. A sample BI blueprint

Note #	Measure	Product	Geography	Customer	Call Class	Sales Rep	Time
			Dimensions				
1	unit sales	product #	region	NA	NA	NA	month
1	amount sales	product #	region	NA	NA	NA	month
1	cost	product #	region	NA	NA	NA	month
1	margin	product #	region	NA	NA	NA	month
2	# calls	product #	district	cust ID	level 1	NA	day
2	call length	product #	district	cust ID	level 1	NA	day
3	unit sales	product #	district	cust ID	NA	rep ID	week
3	amount sales	product #	district	cust ID	NA	rep ID	week
3	unit orders	product #	district	cust ID	NA	rep ID	week
3	amount orders	product #	district	cust ID	NA	rep ID	week
3	commission	product #	district	cust ID	NA	rep ID	week

At this point the brainstorming session (or sessions where multiple departments and complex processes are being reviewed simultaneously) is completed. The group has identified through a process of asking questions the most important measures and their related dimensions for answering the most significant questions agreed on by the group.

Evaluating Alternatives

When the brainstorming process is completed, a smaller group of individuals—minimally a business analyst and an IT or systems expert—synthesizes the information from the BI blueprint into a list of BI opportunity areas for more detailed evaluation. There are four steps in the process of evaluating BI opportunities:

1. Group requirements into opportunity areas.

2. Grade opportunities by importance.

3. Grade opportunities by difficulty.

4. Rank opportunities (including possible return on investment).

Group Requirements into Opportunity Areas

Strictly speaking, the BI blueprint documents the measures and dimensions for answering business questions and reflects the most fundamental requirements for building BI solutions. Clearly, the information in the blueprint needs to be analyzed and fleshed out further outside the rough-and-tumble environment of a brainstorming session. The BI blueprint also has to be reorganized somewhat to reflect a categorization or grouping of the line items of measures and dimensions in opportunity areas that can be individually discussed and evaluated.

In BI technical terms we define **opportunity area** as a logical grouping of measure requirements, where data can be obtained consistently across all the dimensions at the same lowest level of detail. In business terms an opportunity area is a consistent set of requirements for a group of users that can be accommodated more or less from the same end-to-end system structures or solution. Examples of common BI opportunity areas for a large sales organization might include sales management, funnel management, and demand forecasting. Opportunity areas for finance would include financial reporting and budgeting. Typical cross-functional opportunity areas are product contribution analysis and customer/channel profitability.

Table 9-2 is a listing of BI opportunities in various functional areas across several industries. While this is not a comprehensive listing, it does provide an idea of the opportunity areas that may exist in an organization.

Table 9-2. Opportunities by functional areas across industries

	Manufacturing	Retail	Financial Services	Medicine & Health Care	Transportation	Professional Services	Energy	Telecommunications
Finance								
Performance Management	✓	✓	✓	✓	✓	✓	✓	✓
Budgeting	✓	✓	✓	✓	✓	✓	✓	✓
Profitability	✓	✓	✓	✓	✓	✓	✓	✓
Risk			✓	✓	✓			
Fraud		✓	✓	✓				
Balanced Scorecard	✓	✓	✓	✓	✓	✓	✓	✓
Marketing								
Customer Relationship Management	✓	✓	✓	✓	✓	✓	✓	✓
Promotions	✓	✓	✓	✓	✓	✓	✓	✓
Segmentation	✓	✓	✓	✓	✓	✓	✓	✓
Brand Management	✓	✓	✓	✓				
Category Management	✓	✓	✓					
Churn		✓	✓	✓	✓			

Table 9-2.   Opportunities by functional areas across industries (*continued*)

	Manufacturing	Retail	Financial Services	Medicine & Health Care	Transportation	Professional Services	Energy	Telecommunications
Loyalty	✓	✓	✓	✓	✓	✓	✓	✓
Market Basket		✓	✓	✓				
Sales								
Sales	✓	✓	✓	✓	✓	✓	✓	✓
National Account Management	✓	✓	✓	✓		✓	✓	
Sales Funnel Management	✓	✓		✓		✓	✓	✓
Demand Forecasting	✓	✓	✓	✓	✓	✓	✓	✓
Web Analysis	✓	✓	✓	✓	✓	✓	✓	✓
Operations and Supply Chain								
Network Traffic	✓	✓			✓	✓	✓	✓
Yield	✓	✓		✓				
Supply Chain	✓	✓	✓	✓	✓	✓	✓	✓
Vendor	✓	✓	✓	✓	✓	✓	✓	✓
Quality	✓	✓	✓	✓	✓	✓	✓	✓
Customer Service	✓	✓	✓	✓		✓	✓	✓
Human Resources	✓	✓	✓	✓	✓	✓	✓	✓

While the examples from the brainstorming session presented earlier are trivial, Table 9-3 reorganizes the information in Table 9-1 into an opportunity area structure.

Three opportunity areas were created from the raw sticky note information—product margin analysis, sales analysis, and customer support. The process for creating these three areas was strictly analytical, that is, a methodical resolution of the conflicts between the information needs of the measures and dimensions defined by the various sticky note questions.

For example, the organization of the product margin analysis opportunity resulted from the limited dimensionality requirement (only three of the six candidate dimensions) and the higher level time dimension focus (month vs. week or day). The sales analysis opportunity organization is driven by the need for information by sales representative, a unique focus that is really out of step with the product margin and customer support areas, plus the need for a weekly timetable. Finally, and most obviously, the customer support opportunity is driven by the unique character of the measures (# calls and call length), neither of which have much to do with sales, orders, and the like that are measures for the other two opportunity areas. A real-world approach for organizing opportunity areas would involve applying intuition and common business sense as well as pure elimination analysis.

Table 9-3. A sample opportunity area structure based on the data in Table 9-1

| | Dimensions | | | | | |
	Product	Geography	Customer	Call Class	Sales Rep	Time
Product Margin Analysis						
Amount Sales	product #	region	NA	NA	NA	month
Cost	product #	region	NA	NA	NA	month
Margin	product #	region	NA	NA	NA	month
Sales Analysis						
Amount Sales	product #	district	cust ID	NA	rep ID	week
Amount Orders	product #	district	cust ID	NA	rep ID	week
Unit Sales	product #	district	cust ID	NA	rep ID	week
Unit Orders	product #	district	cust ID	NA	rep ID	week
Commissions	product #	district	cust ID	NA	rep ID	week
Customer Support						
# Calls	product #	district	cust ID	level 1	NA	day
Call Length	product #	district	cust ID	level 1	NA	day

Grade Opportunities by Importance

If brainstorming is pushed far enough, the first comprehensive look at business intelligence for a large business unit will yield many opportunity areas in virtually all functional areas of the business, plus a number of very attractive ones across functional areas. To help you rank the importance of each opportunity, here is a quick litmus test based on three criteria: (1) actionability of information, (2) materiality of the impact, and (3) tactical vs. strategic focus. By applying these three criteria, you should be able to assign an overall high, medium, and low priority grade to each opportunity area.

Actionability of Information

For each area determine the **actionability** of the information that would come from the proposed BI solution. While questions such as "Why do we get more support calls from the West Coast than other regions?" may be interesting, a manager having the information probably would not do anything differently if there were no issues of scheduling or shift coverage. By contrast, a critical benefit of the CompUSA solution described in Chapter 6 was the highly actionable nature of the information across the board. Executive and regional managers could quickly spot stores in trouble and jump in to help. Store managers could identify problem employees who needed more training or a reprimand and then take specific action. Store managers could quickly fix processes that were broken, for example, improving procedures for gathering warranty information. Even though the CompUSA solution focused on many low-level details of the business, the system delivered highly actionable information to all levels of management and across all stores in the company.

Actionability of information is scored on a scale of high, medium, or low. BI opportunities that score low on actionability of information can be automatically scored low priority on overall importance of the information. In more blunt terms, forget about opportunities that are not clearly actionable and focus on the ones that can empower people to make a difference in the company.

Materiality of the Impact

For each area, determine the **materiality** of action resulting from the information that would come from the proposed BI solution. Could you make or save a significant amount of money if the information was available on an ongoing basis?

Asking the "what's core to our success" question sometimes leads to the same conclusions. For example, is the functional area or process that would be improved by implementing a BI solution a core competence of the business that provides competitive advantage? Or is the process noncore to your success, in which case it may be good enough as is?

While the Audi AG solution in Chapter 4 was focused on the nuts and bolts of assembly line scheduling and involved seemingly arcane minutia, the solution was highly material to Audi's bottom line, impacting production efficiencies, inventory levels, supplier relations, and customer satisfaction. There is no question that production management at the lowest level is core to Audi. This is not a functional area the company would outsource.

Like actionability of information, materiality of the impact is scored on a scale of high, medium, or low. BI opportunities that are not financially material regardless of actionability should be scored low priority. Noncore activities are a potential flag for such designations.

Tactical vs. Strategic Focus

Think through the opportunity in terms of its *tactical vs. strategic* impact on the business. How does the BI opportunity impact short-term objectives and operating results vs. long-term goals or significant competitive advantages?

While this criterion overlaps the materiality issue discussed in the previous section, the most important impact of business intelligence is frequently strategic in nature, and this positive impact often comes from the simple accumulation of improved decision making by managers and executives who live the BI attitude and work the BI cycle that was described in Chapter 1. The problem, though, is that attitudes, quality of decision making, and the like are hard to measure. Purely strategic BI initiatives require a lot of faith: that the BI system will come together; that users, higher level managers, and executives will really use it; and that people will make better decisions from it. Strategic BI initiatives, while theoretically important, often are a higher risk in implementation without a strong commitment that starts and continues from the top down.

At a more practical level, the indicators of tactical vs. strategic orientation of specific opportunities are characterized as follows:

- The greater the interest and the more frequent the potential use of a BI solution at higher levels of the organization, the more strategic the opportunity to impact the accumulated quality of strategic decisions within the company. Think through and find out who at what organization level will use the BI solution.

- The more cross-functional the requirements and the profile of potential users, the more likely the opportunity will be strategic in nature. BI solutions also tend to be extremely effective at knitting together organizations, resolving disparities about who has the right numbers and analyses, and resolving historical contentious notions of the right things to do. This is clearly true with complex BI applications that link, for example, finance and other departments, such as product contribution analysis, customer/channel profitability analysis, customer relationship management, and financial planning/forecasting.

Of these three criteria, the spectrum of *tactical vs. strategic* impact is less absolute than *actionability* and *materiality*. For example, tactical opportunities should not be automatically scored low priority just because they are tactical; nor should strategic BI opportunities be ranked high priority if systems are already in place to meet the strategic need. It may be difficult to get management focused on strategic BI opportunities if there are "burning bridge" tactical opportunities everywhere.

Finally, as we saw in the CompUSA case study, some larger projects may be designed to meet tactical as well as strategic objectives. The lesson: look hard for opportunities and designs that meet information needs that span many organizational levels and work hard to resolve potential political issues that arise when managers outside a functional area have access to departmental BI information on a continuous basis. The political issues are often difficult to overcome, but many organizations that adopt the true BI attitude make the hurdle.

Applying the Importance Criteria

Table 9-4 shows how we would apply these three criteria to the three opportunity areas defined from the brainstorming session example. For each opportunity area an overall grade of high, medium, or low indicates the overall importance rating.

Table 9-4. Application of importance criteria to opportunity areas

	Actionability	Materiality	Tactical or Strategic	Overall
Product Margin Analysis	High	High	Strategic	High
Sales Analysis	High	High	Tactical	Medium
Customer Support	Low	Low	Tactical	Low

Remember, we are not evaluating the importance of functional areas to the business as a whole. For example, the sales and customer support organizations are likely very core and strategic in their impact on the business—not activities to be farmed out. The evaluations are about the impact of the specific BI opportunities being proposed. If initial evaluations of the importance ratings do not ring true, return to the brainstorming sessions and think about whether the participants understood the BI concepts underlying the questions they asked. Or perhaps the wrong people were in the meeting; or maybe a key person with broader vision and a real BI attitude was absent that day.

Grade Opportunities by Difficulty

Choosing BI opportunity areas that are easier to implement—regardless of how the potential projects rank in importance—is especially important when an organization has little experience with business intelligence. It is important to understand the *difficulty* of each opportunity before proceeding. Therefore, we suggest a quick litmus test for assessing the potential difficulty of implementing an opportunity based on three criteria: cross-functionality of design, existence and accessibility of data, and complexity of calculations. By applying these three criteria, you should be able to assign an overall easy, medium, or hard difficulty grade to each opportunity area.

Cross-Functionality of Design

Cross-functional opportunities are typically more difficult to design and implement than strictly functional or within department opportunities. The principal reason is that people from different departments often view their information needs differently, and reconciling such differences is both time-consuming and political. For example, different departments focus on different measures and dimensions. They often use different terminology and have different requirements for specifying hierarchies within dimensions. For example, the finance and marketing groups often have different conceptions on how to structure product groups and product lines for a product dimension.

The frequent result is a BI design that tends to accommodate the needs of multiple functional groups, that is, designs with more measures, more dimensions, lower levels of detail, and more complex hierarchies. Complexity in these respects is not a bad thing; it just takes more time and hard work to get right. Cross-functional opportunities are given a score of hard. Functional opportunities are given a score of easy.

Existence and Accessibility of Data

To assess the existence and accessibility of data, consider the following three questions:

- *Is there data to support the measures and dimensions?* For example, if the opportunity includes inventory quantity as a measure, is that data available for the dimensions you have chosen, by warehouse, by product, by customer, and by timeframe? (Notice the *by* connectors once again.) If data is missing for a given dimension, for example, customer, you may have to change the dimension specifications, modify the process for gathering the source data, or determine an allocation scheme.

- *Is there data to support the new metrics that have been identified?* Similar to the previous question but more serious, you may specify new measures where the data simply does not exist across any dimension within your data sources. Measuring customer satisfaction is a typical example. Many organizations have not paid attention to this area and have had to put in place completely new processes to gather information about customer attitudes. It is frequently the case that BI initiatives drive the creation of new processes. Such opportunity areas are more difficult, however, because a data collection system must be built from the bottom up.

- *How feasible is the level of detail that was specified?* Sometimes the level of detail specified for the combination of all dimensions results in an overwhelming number of data points that simply cannot be processed within the windows of time available or with the hardware/software configurations within the company's budget. Early in the analysis of opportunity areas, estimate how much data will need to be stored as well as how much new data must be processed with each refresh cycle.

Based on your answers to these questions, rate each opportunity area on a scale of easy, medium, or hard for the availability of data.

Complexity of Calculations

Earlier in the chapter, we differentiated between *base measures,* those that occur naturally in the data, such amount sales and unit sales, and *calculated measures,* those that are calculated from base measures, for example, average price from amount sales divided by unit sales. While relational databases, and OLAP databases in particular, have extensive capabilities for calculating measures across multiple dimensions, the more complex the calculated measures included in the information requirements for an opportunity area, the more difficult the implementation will be.

The complexities of calculated measures can be especially challenging when you are sourcing information from multiple OLTP systems. For example, a customer profitability analysis may include sales, discounts, and pricing information by customer available in the sales order OLTP system, whereas cost data by product (not available by customer) is likely found in the accounting department cost system. This is a typical data population problem found with cross-functional applications that can be solved, but the solution involves complex allocation algorithms and calculated measures that will cause the system to be more complex and therefore more difficult to implement.

From a calculation standpoint the easiest projects to implement are those that assimilate data for base measures from the OLTP systems and roll up the data into hierarchies across each dimension without many calculated measures. The complexity of calculations is scored on a scale of easy, medium, or hard.

Applying the Difficulty Criteria

Table 9-5 applies the difficulty criteria to the three opportunity areas defined as part of the example brainstorming session. (Note: this is an example only. You would typically have much more information about the opportunity areas than has been provided for these areas.)

Table 9-5. Applying the difficulty criteria to three opportunity areas

	Cross-Functional	Availability of Data	Complexity of Calculations	Overall
Product Margin Analysis	Hard	Medium	Hard	Hard
Sales Analysis	Easy	Medium	Easy	Easy
Customer Support	Easy	Easy	Medium	Easy

Difficulty is essentially driven by how cross-functional the opportunity is, the availability of source data, and the complexity of the calculated measures. At this point you will have only a relative hunch for how easy or how hard it will be to build a BI solution that can take advantage of a particular opportunity area. These three considerations are very helpful when performing a quick assessment of the difficulty level of the opportunity areas. During implementation of the BI solution, you will undoubtedly adjust these difficulty ratings as the business requirements are refined and the source data to support the dimensions and measures is located.

Rank Opportunities

The final step is divided in two parts: (1) creating a scorecard for quickly visualizing how different BI opportunities compare and (2) thinking through the costs, benefits, and financial returns of specific opportunity areas.

Creating a BI Opportunity Scorecard

Figure 9-3 depicts a BI opportunity scorecard. The scorecard is a pictorial representation of the opportunity areas that have been evaluated using the criteria of importance and difficulty that you would have developed from the guidelines given in the previous sections.

To build the scorecard, draw a quadrant (as shown in Figure 9-3) on a conference room whiteboard or with a charting program. Number the various opportunity areas (or assign a brief description) and then place each into the appropriate quadrant. This is not a true mathematical plotting. Take advantage of the range between high and low importance and high and low difficulty. The quadrant is a relative gauge for assessing the importance and feasibility of information requirements.

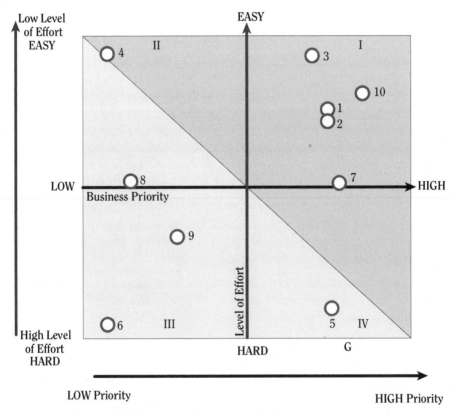

Figure 9-3. *A sample BI opportunity scorecard*

By displaying the information in the format of Figure 9-3, a sense of the relative feasibility of BI opportunities is achieved, including a short list of areas that could be analyzed in terms of development cost, benefits, and financial return. The following guidelines should be used to create the short list:

- *High/easy* opportunities. If there are high-priority opportunities that can be supported by readily available data with straightforward calculations, these are good candidates to evaluate more and start soon.

- *Medium/easy* and *low/easy* opportunities. Weigh the relative value of the opportunities against their difficulty of implementation. Having a couple of easy wins when just starting with business intelligence is often important, even if the opportunity is not a burning bridge.

- *High/medium* and *high/hard* opportunities. When the perceived difficulty is greater because of sourcing or complex calculations but the importance is high, consider doing a **pilot project**. We discuss pilot projects more in Chapter 10. The goal of a pilot project is to limit the resource commitment until you determine how difficult the project will be. A pilot project may be something developed within your organization; alternatively, a professional services firm experienced in building such applications may be hired for the project.

- *Medium/medium* and *low/medium* opportunities. Pilot projects can also be used for medium/medium and low/medium opportunities. Given that these opportunities have a lower priority, there may be less justification and funding for such projects.

- *Medium/hard* and *low/hard* opportunities. It probably does not make sense to invest in medium/hard or low/hard opportunities. Put them aside for now.

Costs, Benefits, and Returns

BI opportunities are typically more difficult to evaluate than other IT projects using traditional return on investment, payback, and discounted cash flow techniques, especially for companies that have no experience with the technologies. OLTP systems are inextricably linked to the day-to-day processes of the business, where costs are generally well known and consequences of systems failures, for example, not processing an order or not invoicing a customer for goods shipped, are understood and easily quantified.

With business intelligence, however, the most important benefits, while intuitively obvious, are often not easily quantifiable in advance. They revolve around less measurable, more esoteric variables, such as the impact of having information sooner, the quality of decisions, new marketplace insights and tactics, and potential shifts in competitive strategy.

This difficulty of assessment is especially true for more complex cross-functional opportunities such as product margin analysis and pricing—that is, basic product profitability and positioning issues—and customer-oriented projects such as customer/channel profitability and customer satisfaction. You know that having good information about products or customers, for example, data that accounts for all costs of manufacturing, marketing, and development, would surely have a large impact on pricing strategies, product offerings, and customer segmentation. Until you do it, though, you can only guess at the financial impact.

Our advice is to document information in quantitative terms up front: not only the hard project costs and cost savings or revenue benefits but the intangible benefits as well. Both long term and short term, the return on investment from business intelligence comes with its aggressive use within the organization and the adoption of a true BI attitude in decision making.

For the project cost component of the analysis, the typical categories to account for include the following:

- Cost of new hardware or the opportunity cost of using current hardware

- Cost of software, including ETL tools, relational and OLAP databases, application packages, and front-end software for users

- Internal development costs—staff and expenses for designing and implementing the BI opportunity

- External development costs—service professionals experienced in BI development (This expense is particularly important when dealing with first-time or complex opportunity areas.)

- Internal training (both business and technical IT staff need to get up to speed on the BI technologies to be used and user training on front-end tools)

- Ongoing maintenance after implementation

Quantifiable or somewhat quantifiable benefits that can be used in the numerator of a return on investment or payback calculation typically include the following:

- Time saved in producing reports

- Operating efficiencies from specific information, for example, the Audi assembly line economics

- Lower investment levels—that is, cost of capital savings—resulting from process improvements such as better inventory or accounts receivable

- Improved customer service and satisfaction and therefore higher revenues from add-on products, services, warranties, replacement business, and so forth

The list of intangible benefits, while difficult to quantify, is where the greatest and fastest paybacks occur.

- Improved operational and strategic decisions from better and more timely information

- Improved employee communications and job satisfaction resulting from a greater sense of empowerment

- Improved knowledge sharing

Summary

When starting a BI initiative, you will often find that there are too many opportunities and not enough time or money. To help you get started, we provided a number of hands-on techniques for identifying BI opportunities. Doing your homework helps you understand the most important information considerations in identifying BI opportunity areas: the functional areas of the organization that will use business intelligence; the users of the intelligence; and the information needed in terms of measures, dimensions, and level of detail.

Next we delivered an organized process for brainstorming information requirements in facilitated sessions, including methods for determining the brainstorming team, asking specific business questions, and turning the questions into specific information requirements for defining measures and dimensions. Brainstorming is an opportunity to hear from the organization and generate general enthusiasm for business intelligence.

In the last section we provided specific guidelines for evaluating BI opportunities: how to group requirements into opportunity areas, criteria for grading opportunities by importance and difficulty of implementation, displaying opportunity areas using a BI opportunity scorecard, and thinking through costs and benefits. At the end of the day, however, business intelligence is one of those investments that has to be tried and used to be understood. The best and fastest justification for second and third BI implementations will be the success of the first one and the enthusiasm of users who will start to feel the power of making better decisions faster.

Implementing a BI Solution

Chapter 9 described how you can accomplish the first goal of the BI roadmap—identifying your most prominent BI opportunities. This chapter describes how you can accomplish the second goal of the BI roadmap—implementing a BI solution to take advantage of your BI opportunities.

A **BI solution** is a way to bring together people, technology, and data to deliver valuable information to business decision makers. Given that a large part of implementing a BI solution involves digging through data and applying BI technologies, you may think that the tasks associated with implementing a BI solution are the responsibility of only technology professionals. While technology experts play a critical role in working through the technical details of the BI solution, business decision makers also play an equally critical role in making sure that the BI solution meets their information and analysis needs.

To help businesspeople work successfully with technical experts, this chapter serves as an implementation guide for business decision makers. The guide is divided into two parts:

- An *implementation strategy* for building a BI solution, using the BI technologies described in Chapter 3.

- The *fundamental decisions* of a BI solution, including practical advice for business decision makers to effectively participate in each decision.

An Implementation Strategy

In Chapter 3 you learned the basic components of the data warehouse system, a flexible and effective platform for supporting an organization's BI initiatives. In this chapter you learn an implementation strategy for applying these components to take advantage of your most prominent BI opportunities. This implementation strategy uses the following high-level guidelines:

- Think big and start small.
- Pay special attention to your first step.
- Assemble the puzzle pieces early.
- Use well-defined BI projects.
- Leverage success again and again.

Let's look more closely at these guidelines to understand why each is critical to the success of your implementation.

Think Big and Start Small

Your list of prominent BI opportunity areas represents the big picture vision of information requirements across various functional areas and business units of your organization. When it is time to build a BI solution to meet these requirements, you need to balance this big picture view with small steps that help you realize your big picture vision one success at a time. Put into practice, "think big and start small" means using the BI opportunity areas to guide the creation of several data marts.

In Chapter 3 you learned that a data mart stores data related to a particular subject of analysis. While there really is no hard and fast rule for determining the subject of a data mart, the following are helpful hints:

- Data marts are typically composed of one or more related opportunity areas. A data mart can address more than one opportunity area when the areas have similar business users, dimensions and measures, or departmental sponsorship. For example, because product margin analysis and sales analysis both relate to sales, you may decide to group these and other related opportunities together into one subject-specific data mart called sales.

- Data marts are typically short-term deployments that can last anywhere from three to six months—sometimes even shorter—to provide you with a return on your investment in a relatively short time frame.

The overall goal is to build these data marts one a time, starting with the one that has the greatest priority and the lowest anticipated effort and then proceeding to the other data marts based on your importance/difficulty rankings. Each data mart is treated as a separate project, with its own budget, timing, and success parameters. At the end of this process, you will have a series of subject-specific data marts that will collectively define your new data warehouse or enhance your existing data warehouse.

Pay Special Attention to Your First Step

Your first data mart is typically the most significant because many people are going to judge the BI solution based on the outcome of the initial endeavor. The success or failure of the first data mart could affect funding of future projects, enthusiasm for business intelligence, and overall adoption for the BI solution by the organization. As a result, you should start with a data mart that you know can be a great success and also one that you can leverage in subsequent data mart deployments.

In addition, expect your first data mart deployment to have more up-front costs than subsequent data marts because you will be investing in tools and technologies, consulting services, and/or internal development efforts. Once the first data mart has been deployed, the incremental costs of building additional data marts tend to be lower because you are expanding on and extending the infrastructure created for the first data mart.

Assemble the Puzzle Pieces Early

Assemble the puzzle pieces of the data mart—dimensions, measures, data, and technology—sooner rather than later. What this means in practical terms is using an iterative or cyclical design approach for building data marts instead of using a linear development approach. By taking this approach, over the course of the implementation, you will produce two or three iterations of the data mart, with each iteration more sophisticated than the previous one; the final iteration is your finished data mart. In contrast, if you use a linear approach, you will not have a working data mart until very late in the development cycle.

An iterative design technique is beneficial for many reasons. The process of building each iteration allows you to work through unforeseen technology, design, or data issues fairly early in the development cycle, thereby reducing the costs of implementing significant architectural changes fairly late in the development cycle. In addition, instead of having business users spend time reviewing hundreds of pages of written documentation that simply regurgitate information requirements, you can show them their requirements in action and validate those requirements using a live version of the data mart. Not only does this allow users to play with something more concrete than sticky notes, but it also gives them a good idea for the look and feel of the BI solution, which can be especially helpful if they are new to interactive, multidimensional analysis.

Use Well-Defined Projects

Having an effectively structured BI project ensures that your BI solution delivers maximum business value to your organization. While no cookie-cutter BI project applies to every company, it is important to realize that there are different types of BI projects depending on what are you trying to accomplish. To help you understand what these options are, three categories of projects will be discussed in the following sections: **pilot projects**, **proof-of-concept projects**, and full-scale projects. Unfortunately, there is no industry standard surrounding these categories, so the terms given here may be different than what you see in other books or hear throughout the industry. Their distinction is important, however, because each project has a different goal and provides you with a different way to take action on your BI opportunities.

Proof-of-Concept Project

The primary goal of a proof-of-concept project is to evaluate and select BI technologies to host your data marts. Most proof-of-concept projects focus on testing the capabilities of back-end OLAP or relational database engines. For example, you may embark on a proof-of-concept project to evaluate how effectively a particular OLAP database technology can meet the requirements of a proposed finance data mart. For this data mart, the ability for hundreds of users to write back their budgeting scenarios is a critical make-or-break feature that the OLAP database needs to support. The proof-of-concept project may be relatively quick if you evaluate only one database vendor; alternatively, it may be fairly involved if you test the capabilities of multiple vendors. To make the proof-of-concept project most effective, however, you should focus on evaluating a short list of vendors, rather than an extended list. The outcome of the proof-of-concept project, along with other technology decisions made outside the project, will determine the final choice of technologies that will be used to build the data marts during the full-scale BI project.

In the "BI Technologies" section of this chapter, you will find evaluation criteria for selecting BI technologies to help guide your proof-of-concept project. You will most likely expand on these criteria to produce a fairly detailed list of the features and functions for a particular BI implementation.

Pilot Project

The primary goal of a pilot project is to test the feasibility of pursuing a specific BI opportunity area. Opportunity areas that are rated high/hard and high/medium are great candidates for pilot projects. Pilot projects are relatively short in duration—approximately two to three weeks in length—in which time you perform tasks to thoroughly assess the difficulty of finding source data to support your dimensions and measures. The final output of the pilot project is a prototype, a small-scale version of the data mart.

Pilot projects are also great opportunities to test the waters of business intelligence in your organization and educate business users about what business intelligence has to offer. Typically, the prototype produced in a pilot project is not considered an official iteration of the data mart development cycle. Many times, the actual prototype is scrapped after it is completed; however, the knowledge gathered about design feasibility is used to determine whether it is beneficial to approach the opportunity area in a full-scale project.

The Full-Scale Project

The goal of a full-scale project is to successfully build and deploy a candidate data mart. To support the implementation guidelines that we have presented in this chapter, we recommend that a full-scale project proceed with following four primary phases.

Phase 1—Investigating and Planning.   One of the first steps in the investigating and planning phase is defining the members of the implementation team. Once the team is identified, the team will conduct a series of interviews with the executives, managers, and analysts who will use the BI solution. The goals of these interviews are to refine the design of the dimensions and measures and identify how various communities of users want to analyze information.

While the dimensions and measures are driven by business requirements, their design must also be grounded in reality, that is, real source data. To verify that their design is realistic, the implementation team starts to hunt down and evaluate whether the source data can support the dimensions and measures. This process will also involve additional interviews with the technical experts who currently manage and assimilate data.

To bring together the design and the data, the implementation team will typically build a preliminary iteration of the BI solution, using the tools and technologies chosen for the project. We believe this iteration to be a critical component of the investigating and planning phase; it allows users to see and interact with the dimensions and measures at an early stage. Obviously, the preliminary iteration will not address every requirement; however, it will allow users to validate their business requirements and provide valuable feedback. It will also generate excitement and clinch their support for your project.

Phase 2—Development.   Of all the project phases, the development phase is probably the longest. With the selected technologies identified, the main goal of the development phase is to develop iterative builds of the BI solution. In this process, business requirements are continually refined, source data that can support the business requirements is gathered and evaluated, design approaches are tested, and the selected database and front-end technologies that can support the design are verified.

Two to three iterations will typically be built during the development phase; each iteration is usually more sophisticated than its immediate predecessor. By more sophisticated, we mean that the design has gone from small data sets to full data volumes and involves the increasing participation of more business users to test each iteration. At the end of this process, the final iteration is the final data mart for the first project.

Phase 3—Go Live and Educate.   During the go live and educate phase, the implementation team flips the magic switch to launch the BI solution. Flipping the switch sounds relatively easy; however, there are a series of prelaunch tasks that need to be addressed before you can ensure that the BI solution takes off successfully. These tasks include educating business users on accessing information from the BI solution, setting up a support infrastructure, and transferring knowledge from the implementation team to support staff.

Phase 4—Measure and Enhance.   The measure and enhance phase typically occurs a few months after the deployment of the BI solution. At this point the task is to measure the success of the project by interviewing users and assessing how well the data mart is meeting their analysis needs. This is also a great opportunity to fine-tune the performance of the BI solution and make additional enhancements that users want. At the end of this phase, you are ready to start the project cycle again to identify and take advantage of additional BI opportunities.

Leverage Each Success Again and Again

Without a strategy to leverage the success of completed data marts and share information among these marts, you may end up creating data silos that do not integrate information together. Creating data silos instead of data marts that share information is a common pitfall that many organizations face when they build data marts. The best way to safely bypass this pitfall is to use the following tips to help you integrate data marts together over the long term:

- Keep track of what data you have and what data you need by cross-checking each data mart's dimensions and measures with your big picture list of BI opportunity areas.

- Use only BI technologies that facilitate the sharing of dimensions and measures across data marts for reporting and analysis.

- Make the organizational commitment to define and resolve definitions of dimensions and measures so that each data mart uses consistent terminology.

- Document contents of each data mart using **metadata**, data that captures the business logic used to build dimensions and measures. You can use this metadata to inform business users about a particular data mart or you can leverage the metadata as you build subsequent data marts. Note that there are BI technologies that are specifically designed to store metadata.

The Fundamental Decisions

To supplement the implementation strategy, the second part of this implementation guide includes practical advice for making the fundamental decisions of the BI solution. These fundamental decisions include selecting the implementation team, choosing BI technologies, deciding on design options for dimension and measures, and handling data issues. Let's examine each of these and describe how a businessperson can play an effective role in each decision.

The Implementation Team

The first fundamental decision is selecting the implementation team. The implementation team is a group of businesspeople and technical experts who work together to translate BI opportunities into a BI solution. As a businessperson, you can either limit your role to participating in the selection of a capable implementation team or participate as an active member of the team. To help you decide who should be on the implementation team, we describe the typical roles and skill sets required to implement a BI solution and offer suggestions for finding the right people to fill those roles.

Executive Sponsor

The executive sponsor of a BI solution supports the implementation both financially and politically. Executive sponsorship is necessary not only for the initial buy-in of the implementation but also for ongoing support. Because a BI solution seeks to improve the status quo and take advantage of new BI opportunities, you should expect some naysayers in your organization, those who fear change and prefer things as they are. Securing the political support from an executive will help generate enthusiasm in the company at large and will also protect the project from the potential sabotage of unsupportive peers. While the executive sponsor is probably not involved in the day-to-day implementation efforts of the solution, to obtain and engage his or her ongoing support, the sponsor should be continuously informed of the progress of the solution, perhaps participating in the review of each iteration of the data mart.

Business Team

The business team actively participates during all stages of the implementation and works hand-in-hand with technical experts to define business requirements, make design decisions, and choose technologies for the BI solution. Because it is usually not logistically possible to actively involve all business users, the business team represents the interests of the greater business user community—the tens, hundreds, or even thousands of business users throughout an organization. Depending on the BI opportunity, the team may consist of people from a particular department or from several different departments. To represent the analysis needs of different business users, the team may also involve a cross-section of executives, managers, and analysts. Over the course of the implementation, other business users may also be involved on a part-time or temporary basis to provide feedback on the various iterations of the data mart.

Having business users participate on an ongoing basis during the development of the data mart is absolutely one of the most important success factors to create and sustain enthusiasm for your BI solution. People will get excited about what is in store for them, and this will help keep the BI momentum alive.

Technical Team

The technical team provides the expertise to successfully build the BI solution. Technical experts are important for two reasons: (1) they have knowledge of the data stored in the company's OLTP source systems and existing decision support systems; and (2) they have special expertise in using BI technologies, such as relational databases, OLAP databases, ETL tools, front-end tools, and data mining. Using technical resources that cover all these skill sets is critical to the success of the BI solution. In addition, at various points in the project, the technical team can expand as necessary to include the help of specialists in hardware, operating systems, networking, Web development, and security.

Data Modelers

Data modelers are specialists who work with the business team and the technical team. They are responsible for gathering requirements from the business team and translating those requirements into a workable design of dimensions and measures. This task requires the modelers to wear many hats. They need to understand the business requirements, how the source data supports the business requirements, and how to customize the data mart design based on a particular database technology or front-end reporting and analysis tool. Sometimes these specialists can be the most valuable resources on the implementation team by bridging business and technical interests.

Project Manager

A project manager manages the day-to-day operations of the implementation, making sure that each data mart is successfully deployed under the time and budget constraints of a project. The project manager plans and keeps the project schedule; manages the tasks necessary to reach milestones; and handles issues related to budget, staffing, and project scope.

Internal vs. External Resources

Now that you have an understanding of the primary roles for the implementation team, the next step is to find people to fill these roles. To do this, consider whether your organization has the necessary resources internally to fill these roles or whether you need to secure the services of an external consulting firm.

Let's address this on a role-by-role basis. The executive sponsor and business team are usually internal to your organization. To supplement your business team, you may decide to enlist the help of management consultants or experts with strong industry/business knowledge to help define KPIs and refine business processes. Depending on the size and skill sets of the IT department, data modelers, technical experts, and the project manager may or may not be internal to your organization. These are roles that can be easily supplemented with external consultants.

It is important to note that the most successful projects are the ones involving collaboration between external consultants and internal resources. Most consulting firms prefer to be involved in projects where they can provide the expertise necessary to deploy a BI solution while working hand-in-hand with internal resources to transfer knowledge throughout the project. This transfer of knowledge from external to internal resources is critical to the long-term management of your BI solution.

BI Technologies

The second fundamental decision is choosing effective BI technologies to support your data marts. Choosing BI technologies typically involves the entire implementation team. The team usually starts by evaluating the existing IT systems of the organization. It is only when these existing systems fail to meet information and analysis needs that it becomes necessary to think about investing in more suitable BI technologies.

When you consider your business needs—the BI opportunities identified in Chapter 9 and the potential for multidimensional analysis at the speed of thought—you need to evaluate whether your current tools and technologies can adequately support the desired solution. As you perform this evaluation, be sure to consider the full extent of BI platform technologies that you have in your organization. All too often, companies have BI technologies in-house that are not being used to their full potential. This might result from a lack of communication, for example, when one business unit does not know about BI technologies being used by another business unit. This might also stem from ignorance, for example, when you don't understand the scope of BI technologies that a vendor has bundled together as part of a complete suite. If you have one of these suites, your company may already own BI technologies and simply not be using them. In both the Frank Russell Company and the Cascade Design case studies (Chapters 5 and 8), we saw companies using OLAP technology that had already been licensed as part of a suite to provide a more flexible reporting and analysis environment for users.

If you need to invest in new technology or expand your existing systems, the following section describes critical criteria that you must consider in order to ensure you get the most long-term value from your investments.

Overall Evaluation Criteria

The technologies selected to host a BI solution should have not only specific relevance to the data mart projects at hand but also greater relevance to the company at large; when possible, the technologies should be leveraged across the entire organization. One way to achieve this leverage is by assessing the interoperability of specific BI technologies. Put simply, **interoperability** is a product's ability to work and interact with other products. This makes the product or system more valuable because you end up with a more "open" BI platform. Open platforms are a better long-term investment because they can be used and reused in many different applications. One way to examine a product's interoperability is by evaluating the published standards it supports. The product should support one or all of the following standards: XML/A, OLE DB for OLAP, OLE DB, and ODBC.

In addition to interoperability, cost is an important consideration when evaluating BI technologies. As we stated in Chapter 9, you are typically going to encounter costs in software, development, and training when implementing a BI solution. When evaluating the cost of these technologies, many organizations go through a process of evaluating the costs and benefits associated with "buying vs. building" a BI solution. (This is common IT consideration for many technology investments, not just business intelligence.)

The two extremes of the "buy vs. build" spectrum as they apply to business intelligence are as follows:

- Buying a packaged BI solution from a software vendor—such as the BI accelerators described later in this chapter to produce a subject-specific data mart

- Building a BI solution from scratch using the database technologies offered by a particular vendor and developing custom ETL programs and/or front-end reporting and analysis interfaces to get data into and out of the data mart

Given the extremes of the spectrum, you will probably not find too many companies at either end. On one hand, you will almost never find a packaged BI solution that meets every analysis need out of the box without any customization. On the other hand, you will rarely find a company that needs to build everything from scratch—that is, all aspects of the solution from handwritten ETL programs to front-end user interfaces. The best approach is typically somewhere in the middle, and buy vs. build decisions need to be made on a case-by-case basis.

To help you in your decisions, here are some perspectives on buying vs. building. A worthwhile packaged BI solution will most likely get you to the 60 percent to 80 percent completion point much faster than a BI solution developed from scratch. As such, these packages tend to offer a quicker time to production. The key to purchasing these packages is to understand how much additional effort is required to make a BI solution 100 percent complete. Finding a complete packaged BI solution that fits your business needs is a great situation to be in. Such a solution, unfortunately, is very unusual. However, an increasing number of organizations have realized that they can purchase several packaged BI components and assemble them into a great overall solution.

Beyond interoperability and cost, there are specific evaluation criteria that relate to each category of BI technologies. To help you make technology decisions, we present some of the most important criteria for each of the major categories of BI technologies discussed in Chapter 3.

Front-End Reporting and Analysis Tools

Of all the BI technology decisions, the choice of front-end tools is the most critical for gaining user acceptance. These are the tools that business users rely on to get the information that they need. Front-end tools tend to have relatively short life spans—typically 10 to 20 months; after that you will probably be considering the cost of an upgrade to a newer version. Also, the cost of the software itself is often dwarfed by the investment required by users to learn to operate the software effectively. Consider both of these sometimes hidden factors as you calculate what the true long-term cost will be.

Recall that, as discussed in Chapter 3, there are three general categories of business users—information users, information consumers, and power analysts—each with its own reporting and analysis needs. As you evaluate front-end tools, you should consider the specific needs of each user community as a separate set of requirements. Most tools stand out in one area or the other, although some will excel in both. For each tool that you consider, you should pay attention to the following criteria:

- *Feature/Functionality:* Evaluate the features of the tool based on the perceived benefit to each user community. For example, to meet ad hoc analysis needs, you can develop a set of required features, including standard slicing, dicing, pivoting, creating calculations on the fly, and performing **write back** to the data mart for budgets and forecasts. To meet reporting needs, you can develop a similar list of important criteria, such as prebuilt report templates, conditional formatting, exception reporting, and charting capabilities.

- *Scalability/Deployability:* The ability of the tool to scale to meet the deployment needs of your organization is another critical area for evaluation. Ideally, the tool will allow users to design reports and administer them over the Internet with a **zero client footprint**, that is, no software is installed on the business user's desktop machine (a thin-client tool). Having a zero client footprint will make the BI solution easier to deploy to more users because the tool will not be constrained by the variety of hardware found in the user community. Be sure to compare this zero client footprint functionality with that of the corresponding "thick client," where software needs to be installed on each business user's desktop machine. Sometimes you will find a large difference in functionality between a thin-client tool and a thick-client tool, so you will need to consider the trade-offs between range of functionality and ease of deployability.

- *Usability:* From a usability perspective, it is important to evaluate how much training will be necessary for users in each community to access and use the information that they need either through reporting or ad hoc analysis. To be most cost-effective, choose tools across all user communities that are intuitive, easy to start up and run, and have a minimal learning curve.

- *Manageability:* The effort required to manage and administer the reports and views that users develop is something that often increases over time. Especially in reporting applications, the administration of reports—which can number in the hundreds or thousands—can pose infrastructure challenges to some reporting tools, necessitating a full-time or part-time administrator. Tools should have some administration component to do this.

- *Customization:* The ability to programmatically customize the front-end tool is quite valuable because it allows you flexibility in extending the tool to meet your needs, such as restricting a user's focus or enabling tighter integration into the overall application.

OLAP and Relational Databases

While it is relatively easy to substitute front-end tools, it is not as easy to substitute the back-end database technologies that host the data marts. As a result, the investment in a back-end database technology—OLAP databases and relational databases—is typically long term. This means that you need to pay special attention to what you are looking for in a back-end database to ensure that the BI solution meets both your short-term and long-term analysis requirements.

Even though you may not get involved in the nitty-gritty of the back-end architecture, you should be familiar with the typical criteria the implementation team will use for evaluating back-end database technologies.

While OLAP and relational database technologies have distinct feature sets that you need to assess, the following criteria apply for evaluating both OLAP and relational databases:

- *Scalability:* Both OLAP and relational databases need to be able to handle the number of users and data volumes that you currently have and anticipate to have in the future. Because this is a long-term investment, you want your databases to last for a while and scale to handle growth in the number of users and the volumes of data. In OLAP databases, scalability limits can be measured by analyzing, for example, the number of dimensions, the number of members in each dimension, the number of levels in each dimension, or the number of cubes that the OLAP database can support.

- *Performance:* Both OLAP and relational databases need to support your performance goals. Performance goals can be divided into two categories: data processing speed and data retrieval speed. Of the two, data retrieval performance is the most important because it is most visible to business users who want data to be quickly displayed in their front-end tools in order to support analysis at the speed of thought. With that said, you should not neglect the importance of data processing. Efficient data processing will ensure that the data is ready for users when they need it.

- *Manageability:* Coupled with performance, both OLAP and relational databases need to have a mechanism to manage and tune the database engines as necessary. The technical team should pay special attention to this category.

- *Security:* Both OLAP and relational databases need to have a mechanism to administer security to make sure the right group of people has access to the right data. Also, security should make sure groups of users don't have access to data they should not see. You will typically find lots of variations in the degree of complexity in security implementations.

- *Availability:* Both OLAP and relational databases need to meet availability needs to ensure that the system is up and running when it needs to be and that it is backed up and ready to be restored when something goes wrong.

- *Customization:* Both OLAP and relational databases need to allow programmers to customize and extend the databases as necessary to support specific data storage and administration needs.

- *Write back:* Relational databases provide great capabilities for users to enter updates. It is important to note that many OLAP databases are very weak on this score. Since many BI analysis applications are "read only," this is often not an important consideration. But in those specific cases—such as budgeting and forecasting applications—

where it is an important consideration, the need for write back will have a strong impact on product selection for both the back-end database technology and the front-end reporting and analysis tool.

- *Real Time:* Relational databases provide great support for essentially real-time access to the latest information. As updates are performed, subsequent queries automatically reflect these updates. OLAP technologies typically require a process whereby the raw data is aggregated into a structure that has been optimized to support multidimensional queries. This aggregation delay—which may be long— presents a barrier to those situations where up-to-date information is required. In spite of this barrier, there are successful approaches and designs that can meet the real-time challenge; however, they tend to require significant expertise to implement. At the end of the day, the need for real-time OLAP is really quite unusual for most BI implementations and is therefore rarely considered as a high-priority category in product selections.

ETL Tools

A significant portion of implementation efforts focuses on the extracting, transforming, and loading of data from source systems into the data warehouse. To assist the technical team in implementing ETL processes, a category of software tools, simply called ETL tools, exists to offer productivity enhancements to these processes. Business users will typically not have much interaction with ETL tools. Rather, they will see only the end product of their efforts—cleansed, consistent, and integrated data that is delivered to them in the time frames that they need. The following are some categories that the implementation team should typically use to evaluate ETL tools:

- *Read any source:* ETL tools pride themselves on being able to read data from virtually any source system, such as relational databases, spreadsheets, and data files.

- *Efficiency:* ETL tools routinely process mountains of source data in a fast and efficient manner. Depending on your particular application, this could mean millions or billions of transaction data records.

- *Cross platform:* ETL tools allow programs to be written once and then deployed to a large variety of hardware and operating system platforms.

- *Productivity:* ETL tools provide modern drag-and-drop graphical interfaces to facilitate the development of ETL programs. To increase productivity, these tools typically provide prebuilt transformations that are customized for loading data into a data warehouse.

BI Accelerators

Recently there has been a new genre of applications in the data warehousing space that allow organizations to rapidly build and deploy data marts in a manner that provides an immediate return on investment. Known by many different names, including BI accelerators and analytical applications, this software takes the idea of the prebuilt application, something formerly restricted to operational systems only, and applies it to business intelligence.

More specifically, BI accelerators offer a predefined set of dimensions and measures to address the analysis needs of particular functional area and/or vertical industry. The predefined measures are often industry-accepted KPIs for analyzing specific areas of a business with descriptive dimensions to provide the appropriate context. Examples of BI accelerators include sales and marketing analytics, retail analytics, finance analytics, and others. Because they tend to focus on a narrow subject of analysis, they are sometimes applicable to a single industry only. For example, one analytic application offering may provide the means for hospitals to measure consumer satisfaction—clearly a very narrow focus.

What BI accelerators do well is offer organizations the ability to quickly jump-start a BI solution. By offering packaged data marts that contain OLAP and relational database components, ETL components, and business reporting and analysis components, implementers can spend less time on the common development tasks of a data mart and can spend more time on customizing the data mart to meet the specific analysis needs of a company. As a result, BI accelerators help your organization get a BI solution up and running in a short time frame with significant cost savings.

When considering BI accelerators, it is important to make sure that they are constructed in a manner that is compatible with your company's overall BI strategy. Most analytical applications can integrate quite naturally with whatever flavor of a data warehouse exists in an organization. As such, it is especially important to select BI accelerators that are built on a solid technical framework so that an additional island of data is not created.

Dimension Design

Designing dimensions that meet your analysis needs is another fundamental decision. In Chapter 9 you developed a blueprint to summarize and organize the measures and dimensions that you want (see Table 10-1). The blueprint is an excellent tool to trigger discussions about the dimensional design of your data mart. Business decision makers need to be aware of the multitude of design options that exist for dimensions, including how dimensions are organized into hierarchies, what descriptive attributes support these dimensions, and which dimensions undergo frequent changes.

Table 10-1. A sample blueprint

	Dimensions					
	Product	**Geography**	**Customer**	**Call Class**	**Sales Rep**	**Time**
Product Margin Analysis						
Amount Sales	product #	region	NA	NA	NA	month
Cost	product #	region	NA	NA	NA	month
Margin	product #	region	NA	NA	NA	month
Sales Analysis						
Amount Sales	product #	district	cust ID	NA	rep ID	week
Amount Orders	product #	district	cust ID	NA	rep ID	week
Unit sales	product #	district	cust ID	NA	rep ID	week
Unit orders	product #	district	cust ID	NA	rep ID	week
Commissions	product #	district	cust ID	NA	rep ID	week
Customer Support						
# Calls	product #	district	cust ID	level 1	NA	day
Call length	product #	district	cust ID	level 1	NA	day

The business team should actively participate in identifying the primary components of a dimension's design. Data modelers and the technical team can help guide the business team through this process, but the process needs to be driven by the business requirements. The better the business team understands the design options on the table, the better the final design will be. So read on as we explain each of these design options in detail.

Levels

Hierarchies enable you to perform top-down analysis by drilling down from the most summarized views of data to the least summarized views. Levels are the components of a hierarchy that make this drill down possible. The blueprint documents the lowest level of detail that you want to see for each dimension, that is, the least summarized data. From this starting point, you can begin to think about the other levels that you want to see for each dimension. For example, let's say that you want to analyze sales data by time. The lowest level of detail that you may be interested in is sales for a particular day, but you or other users may also want to see sales data summarized by month, by quarter, and by year. Given these requirements, the complete hierarchy for this dimension is day, month, quarter, year—note that we organized these levels from least summarized to most summarized.

One of the challenges that you face when defining a hierarchy is to decide when something is a level or when it is a completely different dimension. There is a simple test to figure this out; you just need to think about how you want to browse the data.

Table 10-2.   Dimension test: products and years

	2001	2002
Apples	1000	2000
Pears	3500	3000
Grapes	1200	5000
Coffee	500	1000
Tea	700	2200

Consider Table 10-2 as a dimension test. This view of the data seems to make sense. The years have been displayed in the columns, individual products are given in the rows, and sales dollars are at the intersection of each year and each product. For any given pair of entities, there is a given data point. We definitely have two distinct dimensions—time and product.

Now consider Table 10-3. Would you ever want to analyze sales with products on the rows and product categories in the columns? It really does not make much sense to put two related entities on different axes.

Table 10-3. Dimension test: products and product categories

	Fruit	Drinks
Apples	3000	
Pears	6500	
Grapes	6200	
Coffee		1500
Tea		2900

When it does not make sense to split something across axes, it is reasonable to assume that the pair actually represents levels of the same dimension. In this case, individual products and categories belong to the same dimension—product. The dimension's hierarchy therefore consists of two levels: individual product and product category, where individual products roll up into categories.

By applying this simple test, you can quickly identify the difference between levels and dimensions. However, there is a trap to avoid here.

Table 10-4. Dimension test: quarters and years

	2001	2002
Quarter 1	1200	2800
Quarter 2	2600	3700
Quarter 3	1700	3600
Quarter 4	1400	3100

Let's consider Table 10-4. Does this chart make sense? Yes, it does. Are these separate dimensions? No, they aren't. Quarters on the rows and years on the columns may seem like two dimensions; however, time is an example of a special case when the two-axis test does not work. The reason this view makes sense for time is because the quarters are the same from year to year; it also applies to months, weeks, and so forth. It did not make sense in the previous example of individual products and categories because each category had a unique set of products.

Given the results of this test, if you were to design quarters and years as two separate dimensions, you would be sacrificing an important aspect of multidimensional analysis—the ability to drill down. As you learned in Chapter 2, the definition of drill down is the ability to easily navigate through the levels of a dimension's hierarchy. Whenever you make something a separate dimension, you need to make sure that you are not losing any drill-down capabilities. In addition, the more dimensions that you add, the more complex and unwieldy your cube will be.

There are also situations when identifying specific levels in a dimension is not an obvious task. Instead of thinking in terms of levels, it is easier to think in terms of a common relationship. For example, consider a company's organizational chart. Jane, the CEO, is at the top of the organizational chart. Jim, the Vice President of Sales, reports to Jane. Five regional managers report to Jim, and each regional manager has a full staff of sales representatives and administrative personnel. When you try to identify the levels of an organizational chart, it becomes a bit complicated. However, there is common relationship between an employee and a manager. Thinking in terms of this relationship, it is possible to design a dimension to accommodate employees at all levels of an organizational chart, whether they have ten levels of direct reports or no direct reports. This dimension has a special name—a parent-child dimension.

Now that you understand levels, review the dimensions you identified on your own blueprint. Determine how many levels each dimension should have and provide a name for each of these levels. The implementation team will need this information when it is time to build the relational and/or OLAP database components that will support your data mart.

Hierarchies

Once the list of levels has been determined, think about how they can be arranged into a hierarchy. A hierarchy can be assembled by listing the levels from least summarized to most summarized. For example, customers roll up into regions, which roll up into countries. In this case the customer dimension would contain three levels: customer, region, and country.

As you define the levels of the hierarchy, you will most likely have situations when users want to see data summarized by more than one hierarchy. This is perfectly normal. Consider the following example. Let's say that the lowest level of detail to be included in the time dimension is day. The business users decide that they want to see daily data summarized by both fiscal periods and calendar periods. Fiscal periods and calendar periods are really different ways for viewing data by time.

To address this need, you will simply define two time hierarchies: calendar period and fiscal period. The levels in the fiscal hierarchy are day, month, fiscal quarter, and fiscal year. The levels in the calendar hierarchy are day, month, calendar quarter, and calendar year. Are fiscal period and calendar period actually different dimensions? Let's go back to our basic test to find out. Table 10-5 presents fiscal period and calendar period split across two axes. Assume that the fiscal period begins in July.

Table 10-5. Dimension test: calendar period vs. fiscal period

		Calendar Period	
		2001	**2002**
	2000	3800	
Fiscal	2001	3100	6500
Period	2002		6700

It is pretty confusing to split these across the axes of a table. When you analyze data by fiscal period or calendar period, you will want to view the data by one hierarchy or the other—not both at the same time—hence the need for more than one hierarchy. When you have more than one hierarchy in a dimension, the dimension is said to contain alternate hierarchies for viewing data.

Once again, review the dimensions you identified on your blueprint. Decide if any of the dimensions require an alternate hierarchy. If so, define the levels to be contained in each hierarchy and provide a name for each hierarchy.

Attributes

In addition to hierarchies, there will also be other descriptive information that does not directly participate in the hierarchy—in other words, nonhierarchical information. This descriptive information is known as attributes or member properties. Examples of attributes include colors that describe your products or gender and age that describe your customers. Attributes can be an important part of the analysis because they allow you to group and filter data. For example, you can isolate the analysis to look only at sales data where the products are a certain color or a certain size. Attributes can also store additional pieces of helpful information, such as a customer's phone number, address, or fax number. Depending on the underlying technology, attributes can sometimes be their own dimensions.

Consider each dimension in the blueprint and the levels you have identified. You will need to decide if the addition of attributes will enhance analysis, and if so, make a note of them.

Changes

After you have a good understanding of your dimensions, hierarchies, and attributes, you need to consider how dimensions may change over time. Consider the following example. When a salesperson moves from Chicago to Seattle, how should the dimension hierarchy reflect this change and how should the sales for that representative be allocated over time? Should all the historical sales for that salesperson be allocated to the Seattle office or should the history be separated for Chicago and Seattle, respectively? Most likely you will want the history to be maintained as is—all sales before the move go to Chicago and all sales after the move go to Seattle.

Let's consider some other examples. What happens when the phone number for one of your customers changes? In most circumstances you probably just want to replace the old phone number with the new one. Maintaining a historical listing of phone numbers will probably be more trouble than it is worth. However, what happens when a customer has a change in marital status? This may be a tougher call. It really depends on your data analysis needs. You may or may not care about maintaining the history; it depends on whether you need to analyze the buying patterns of your customers based on marital status.

From both business and technical standpoints, the changes that dimensions encounter are an important aspect of dimension design—so important that they have been given a special name: **slowly changing dimensions**. Technical experts have many techniques up their sleeves to handle slowly changing dimensions. As a businessperson, you need to (1) understand which and how often the attributes and the members of each level change over time (any dimension that involves people such as customers and employees is a dimension that will probably undergo significant change) and (2) decide how you want to view the changed data and communicate that information to the technical team.

Measure Design

In addition to selecting design choices for dimensions, another fundamental decision is identifying measure design. There are many design options for measures related to how measures are calculated, how they should be aggregated to higher levels of detail, and how much history is to be stored.

Calculations

The blueprint identifies the measures in which you are interested. Using the blueprint, you can take the design of measures to the next level by defining the specifics behind any calculated measures. From a business perspective, it is necessary to achieve a consensus on how a measure is to be calculated. As we stated previously, this is often a top-down mandate. However, some calculations may be slightly more complicated than required, such as allocations, currency conversions, and cash flow, so it is important to think carefully through the business logic. These can also pose some challenges for the technical team when they build the necessary computations behind the scenes.

Aggregation Method

Once the specifics behind the measures have been defined, think about how each measure should be aggregated across each dimension. This means deciding how the data should be summarized at different levels of detail. Depending on what your business needs are, there are several distinct ways (categories) to control how data is aggregated from its lowest level of detail to its highest level of detail. These categories are **uniform aggregation**, **semiadditive aggregation**, and **custom aggregation**.

- In uniform aggregation, data can be aggregated the same way from the lowest level to highest level across all dimensions. The most common example of uniform aggregation is addition. For example, how are sales dollars per day aggregated to sales dollars for a year? Basically, you add up all the sales for each day to get a total for the year. Other examples of uniform aggregation include counts, distinct counts, averages, and minimum/maximum functions.

- In semiadditive aggregation, measures cannot be aggregated uniformally across all dimensions. For example, in an inventory application, you may measure the inventory value by product, by warehouse, and by time. To calculate the total value of the inventory for all products at a specific warehouse, you can easily add up the inventory value for every product stored in that warehouse. However, if you want to calculate the final inventory value for October of this year, it really does not make sense to add up the value for the 31 days of that month. Rather, the correct answer is the value on October 31st. This type of measure is called a semiadditive measure because you can add the measure across all dimensions except for time. Other examples of semiadditive measures are opening balance and closing balance—or any balance sheet items in financial applications—and headcount in human resources applications.

- Custom aggregations are very powerful ways to handle measures that aggregate differently across different levels of a dimension. To apply custom aggregations, you can use basic mathematical operators or more complex formulas. Consider a chart of accounts dimension shown here:

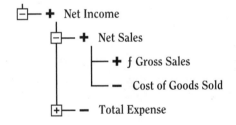

In order to calculate net income, you need to subtract total expenses from net sales. To calculate net sales, you need to subtract the cost of goods sold from gross sales, where the gross sales amount requires a special calculation. Custom aggregations tend to be more complex than uniform or semiadditive aggregations, but they allow you to have lots of control over data summarization.

Refresh and History

The final important design decision for measures is specifying the **refresh rate** and the historical data requirements. The refresh rate is usually identical to the lowest level of detail needed for a time dimension. For example, if you want to analyze sales data on a daily basis, your sales data needs to be refreshed on a daily basis. The second part of this decision is to determine how much history is required to perform meaningful analysis over time. To perform meaningful analysis, you will typically need easy access to a few years of historical data. Once you decide how many years of history are needed, the next question is, "What level of detail is required for all years of historical data?" For example, do you need daily data stored for the last five years or do you need only daily data for the current year and the previous year, and then monthly data summarized for all other years? Keeping data around at low levels of detail for many years can create a large burden for data storage. So be sure that the amount of history that you want is truly something that you are going to use to perform meaningful analysis.

Source Data

As you hammer out design details, you will also need to make decisions regarding source data. Your design can become real only when the necessary source data exists to support your dimensions and measures. Business decision makers do not need to be involved in the details of determining where and how data is stored. Rather, the technical team typically has the job of hunting down the necessary source data to support the design. However, you should not be completely removed from this process; the business team is responsible for making decisions and judgment calls when situations arise where the data cannot support all the business requirements.

While gathering source data may sound like a relatively easy task, it can be quite a challenge to investigate, evaluate, and integrate data from multiple data sources into the desired dimensions and measures. In most circumstances, proceeding from a whiteboard list of dimensions and measures to fully populated data can represent 60 percent to 80 percent of your BI implementation efforts. So what makes this process so challenging, and how can you effectively and efficiently meet these challenges? The answer can be found by examining three critical tasks that are a part of the source data hunt: identifying data sources, evaluating the source data, and handling data issues.

Identifying Data Sources

Identifying data sources is often the first step of the source data hunt. Each dimension and measure needs a data source that can supply the necessary data. These data sources can be OLTP systems, such as the ones described in Chapter 2. They can also be external data sources, such as demographic data purchased from third-party data providers.

Spreadsheets are sometimes listed as candidate data sources, especially in companies that rely on spreadsheets to serve as both desktop data stores and reporting tools. Spreadsheets are typically not ideal data sources because they tend to contain massaged or manipulated data that originated from someplace else. When someone identifies a spreadsheet as a data source, however, do not dismiss it. It is a good idea to analyze the logic contained in the spreadsheets and talk to the people who created and/or use the spreadsheets in order to understand where they got the data in the first place. Once the proper data source is identified, whatever manipulation logic that the spreadsheet performs on the data needs to be documented and transferred to the data mart's ETL processes.

Understanding and documenting this logic may be no small feat. Some of the spreadsheets that companies have used over the years may have become quite complex in the depth and level of calculations and manipulations that they perform. The business team can definitely facilitate this process by helping to explain and streamline the spreadsheet logic. You may even find mistakes in the spreadsheet logic that you want to correct! At the end of the day, it will definitely be worth the effort to build the data mart using the extracted data from the original data source and to develop automated programs to perform the necessary manipulations.

Note that there may also be situations when spreadsheet data is actually not captured anywhere else; in other words, the data comes from the brain of the business analyst. An example of this is when spreadsheets are used for planning, budgeting, forecasting, and what-if modeling. In these situations a typical process is for businesspeople to perform several rounds or iterations of number manipulation before deciding which final values to publish. The appropriate solution for these types of business scenarios is to make sure that your data mart that supports something called write back—the ability for business users to read and write data back to the data mart. When you find out that you need write-back capabilities, you will also need to make sure that you have both the necessary back-end database and front-end tools to support it. Recall that this criteria was noted in the "BI Technologies" section of this chapter.

In efforts to identify data sources, you may find out that your organization is not capturing all the data that you need for analysis. In this case, you need to either forgo the business requirements related to that data or make some serious decisions about how you can improve your existing OLTP systems to capture the data or change the business process to store this data in a separate system.

Evaluating Data Sources

Once data sources are identified, the technical team will evaluate them to make sure that they will effectively support your design. The following is a list of the top three evaluation categories that the technical team may use to evaluate data sources:

- *Ability of source data to support dimensions and measures:* This category evaluates how well the source data will support the design of each dimension and measure. Examples of tasks used to perform this evaluation include mapping each dimension and measure to one or more data sources and identifying any specific challenges associated with merging the data sources.

- *Ability of source data to support refresh and history requirements:* This category assesses the feasibility of the data refresh requirements. Examples of tasks used to perform this evaluation include estimating data volumes based on the lowest level of detail required and comparing the refresh rate to the anticipated amount of time required to process the data.

- *Data quality:* This category evaluates the cleanliness of each data source. Examples of tasks used to perform this evaluation include sampling data, identifying how often a particular field is missing data or contains invalid data, and flagging potential problem areas.

Handling Data Issues

Based on the outcome of the technical team's evaluation of the source data, the business team will most likely need to make judgment calls in situations where the data cannot support all the business requirements. Here are some common situations when the business team needs to be involved:

- *Source data does not support dimensions and measures.* You will undoubtedly run into situations when compromises will have to be made, such as postponing or eliminating specific dimensions and measures because the source data does not effectively support them. If it is a matter of tackling the easy wins and postponing the rollout of more difficult dimensions and measures, sometimes this is the best way to ensure that you continue on the path of producing something of value in a relatively short period of time. However, before you completely eliminate measures and dimensions, be sure that you understand why the source data is not there to support it. As we stated earlier, perhaps this is something that your company needs to store on a regular basis.

- *Frequency of data refresh may pose a significant technical challenge.* If the technical team believes that there is a potential issue with meeting the refresh requirements, look closely at the limitations that are causing this issue. For example, is the issue that you cannot have access to the source system on a regular basis or is it a technical limitation? Each of these requires a different approach to resolve the problem—perhaps some political leverage needs to be used to gain less restrictive access to the source system or perhaps it is time to upgrade database technology to something that can better handle the refresh requirements. The bottom line is that you should not simply drop your requirements without understanding what the bottleneck is and if there is a workable solution.

- *Source data is dirty.* If the technical team finds that a particular data source contains lots of invalid or missing data, you need to make some decisions about how to handle the dirty data. The most straightforward way to correct dirty data is to change it in the original source system. When correcting dirty data in the source system is not possible, it becomes necessary to consider ways to apply ETL routines to clean up the data. Sometimes, the best way to raise an issue with dirty data is to publish it! Putting missing data into unknown or not applicable buckets, for example, is a great way to see what data has missing pieces. If you are trying to analyze sales by sale representative and 70 percent of your sales orders have a missing or null sales representative, this is a good indication that you need to contact the right people in your organization who can find out why this field is missing in the source system and how the situation can be resolved.

- *Source data is inconsistent.* If the technical team finds that a particular dimension has multiple data sources that inconsistently represent the dimension data, you will need to make some decisions about which data source will serve as the system of record for the dimension. For example, if your legacy order entry system has a different product hierarchy than your brand new order entry system, you need to decide how to bring this data together into a consistent view. If you adopt the new product hierarchy, this means that ETL routines must map the legacy sales data to the new product hierarchy.

Summary

A successful BI solution is one that sufficiently fulfills the information requirements and analysis needs of business decision makers. The key to a successful BI solution is having an implementation strategy that permits your organization to think big and start small with subject-specific data marts; arranges for an initial data mart success that generates enthusiasm for business intelligence; produces several iterations of a data mart before it is finalized; uses well-defined BI projects; and leverages the success of each data mart deployment.

The up-front and ongoing participation of the business community during the development of a BI solution is also critical to its success. When they serve as members of the implementation team, business decision makers can actively participate in several fundamental decisions of the BI solution, such as selecting members of the implementation team; choosing suitable BI technologies; specifying dimension design options related to hierarchies, levels, and attributes; determining how measures should be calculated and aggregated across all their dimensions; and making judgment calls when there are gaps between the source data and their ideal design.

Conclusion

The key to winning in the Information Age is making decisions that are consistently better and faster than the competition—survival of the fittest. Business intelligence is an approach to managing your business that is dedicated to providing competitive advantage through the execution of fact-based decision making. At a tactical level, business intelligence allows you to achieve this goal by applying a decision-making cycle of analyzing information, gaining insight, taking action, and measuring results. At a strategic level, business intelligence allows you to use the results of your analysis to create superior corporate strategies that outsmart your competitors.

Business intelligence essentially means putting relevant information at the fingertips of decision makers at all levels of your organization—functional areas, business units, and executive management. Technologies exist today to make this possible for all companies—large and small.

As we look to the near future, we find ourselves entering the age of business intelligence for the masses. Wide-scale deployments of BI solutions to thousands of users are currently exceptions but will become the norm for two primary reasons:

- Organizations will realize that there are benefits to gain from empowering their employees with actionable information.

- Business intelligence will become an increasingly cost-effective investment.

Technologies that offer quick deployment and ease of use for businesspeople continue to be the major determinants of which solutions achieve major market success.

Coupled with the age of business intelligence for the masses, we are also entering the age of interoperability. Because technologies are changing rapidly, much of the technology discussion in this book will probably look out-of-date in just a few short years. However, visionary vendors that build products with open platforms that can be leveraged for years to come will continue to offer products with the most value over the long term.

The BI technologies available to organizations become valuable only when they are used to positively impact organizational behavior. Business intelligence is certainly as much about people and culture as it is about business and technology. Having strong leadership at the helm of BI initiatives is critical to achieving the support and confidence of your business decision makers. Those organizations that define and execute an overall plan or roadmap to guide their BI efforts are less likely to spend millions of dollars running down dead ends and are more likely to achieve BI success.

Successful BI initiatives provide businesspeople with the information they need to do their jobs more effectively. Helping people do their jobs better not only benefits your organization but also makes their work lives more rewarding. We all want to be a part of the winning team and contribute to organizational successes in our own distinctive ways. It is this joy of business intelligence that fuels the demand for broader reach across the organization—the report that took seven days to create now takes less than two minutes, the ability to confidently answer questions in meetings because you are prepared with all the facts and figures, and the capability to turn creative visions into concrete solutions. Business intelligence empowers you to achieve all this and much more. What you accomplish is ultimately in your control!

Microsoft Data Warehousing Framework

Microsoft's platform and tools for business intelligence are structured around a concept called the Microsoft Data Warehousing Framework. This appendix is intended to provide readers with a brief overview of the Microsoft Data Warehousing Framework and its components. This framework offers a comprehensive infrastructure for BI applications based on Microsoft SQL Server 2000, SQL Server Analysis Services 2000, and Microsoft Office. More complete information on the BI products from Microsoft is available at *www.microsoft.com/sql.*

SQL Server

The Microsoft Data Warehousing Framework encompasses several Microsoft technologies, but the centerpiece is SQL Server 2000, which delivers an analysis platform and application programming interfaces (APIs) to build tools. SQL Server allows an organization to sort through volumes of information and extract business intelligence—knowledge that people in the organization can use to make better decisions. The main features of SQL Server are the SQL Server Relational Database Engine, Data Transformation Services, Analysis Services, Meta Data Services, and English Query.

SQL Server Relational Database Engine

Relational databases are one of the most effective methods to organize data in a database, and data warehouses use relational database technology as the foundation for their design, construction, and maintenance. In a relational database, data is collected into tables, each of which represents a class of objects that concerns an organization, such as employees and suppliers. The columns of each table represent an attribute of the object represented by the table. For example, an employee table might have columns for attributes such as first name, last name, employee ID, and so on. Each row represents an instance of the object represented by the table. Tables can be defined in many ways, and relational database theory defines a process called normalization, which ensures that the set of tables you define will organize your data effectively.

The core component of SQL Server 2000 is a powerful and full-featured relational database engine, which is used in online transaction processing (OLTP) systems to store the intermediate data stores used when transforming OLTP data for storage in the data warehouse or data mart and to store and manage the data in a data warehouse or data mart. SQL Server 2000 provides many tools for design and manipulation of relational databases, regardless of the applications for which the databases are used. Information about the numerous relational database management tools is provided throughout the SQL Server 2000 documentation.

Data Transformation Services

A data warehouse holds historic data about operations of an enterprise (not current or operational data). In addition, data external to the business (such as industry analyses and stock market news) can be incorporated to provide a complete view of the business or customer. To move organizational data and other data to a data warehouse, organizations need reliable and powerful tools that can move, clean and reformat, and manage this data.

Data Transformation Services (DTS) provides the functionality to import, export, and transform data. The OLE DB architecture of DTS enables companies to copy and transform data from a variety of data sources, including SQL Server and Oracle directly, using native OLE DB providers; ODBC (open database connectivity) sources, using the Microsoft OLE DB Provider for ODBC; Microsoft Access; Microsoft Excel; Microsoft Exchange Server; Microsoft Active Directory; IBM AS/400, DB2, IMS, and VSAM via an OLE DB provider and services in Host Integration Server; and other data sources provided by third-party vendors.

Using DTS, it is possible to populate data warehouses and data marts in SQL Server by importing and transferring data from multiple, heterogeneous sources interactively or automatically, both as needed and on a regularly scheduled basis; create custom transformation objects that can be integrated into third-party products; and access applications using third-party OLE DB providers. DTS allows applications for which an OLE DB provider exists to be used as sources and destinations of data. Significant enhancements to DTS make it easy to import, export, and transform data from a wide range of sources, including text-only files.

A DTS package is an organized collection of connections, tasks, transformations, and workflow constraints assembled programmatically or with a DTS tool and saved to an SQL Server 2000 database, an SQL Server 2000 Meta Data Services database, a structured storage file, or a file intended for use with Microsoft Visual Basic. Using DTS tools to build DTS packages graphically, or by programming a package with the DTS object model, organizations can create custom data movement solutions tailored to specialized business needs.

Analysis Services

When Microsoft added OLAP Services to SQL Server 7.0, it became easier for organizations of all sizes to extract business intelligence from raw data. SQL Server Analysis Services 2000 significantly extends the OLAP functionality of SQL Server 7.0 to provide an end-to-end platform for analysis. Designed for use by business analysts, database administrators, and application developers, Analysis Services allows anyone with SQL and Visual Basic, Microsoft Visual C++, or similar programming experience to use OLAP tools to create custom analysis applications.

SQL Server's OLAP functionality is seen in several ways. Powerful dimension structures enable your cubes to reflect any kind of data or organizational structure, thus simplifying subsequent reporting. "What if" analysis and cube and dimension write back allow interaction with the data and close the loop on the results. Actions, user-defined functions, and drill-through capabilities extend the analysis and reporting to perform other functions based on your data, thus giving your BI system more power and interaction with the rest of your organization.

Two features in particular—linked OLAP cubes and Hypertext Transfer Protocol (HTTP) access to cubes—give SQL Server 2000 the ability to offer powerful Web-enabled data analysis—that is, an analysis performed over the Web. In addition to enabling an organization to extend analysis capabilities to partners outside its firewall, these features create opportunities to sell access to databases to customers over the Web. Another innovation, Extensible Markup Language for Analysis (XML/A), is a data access protocol that extends the Microsoft BI strategy to the Microsoft .NET platform, allowing application developers to provide analytical capabilities to any client that supports XML/A, on any device or platform, using any programming language.

Microsoft OLAP Actions, a new feature of Analysis Services, extends the power of business analysis with functionality that allows users to automatically apply derived conclusions to business processes—a procedure known as **closed-loop analysis**. SQL Server 2000 can also be extended through third-party analysis tools that enhance the power and functionality of Analysis Services.

In SQL Server 2000, Analysis Services introduces data mining, which can be used to discover information in OLAP cubes and relational databases. In data mining, the computer sifts through data to find structures that can be used to describe some aspect of the data or predict future outcomes. Microsoft, with the input and collaboration of its partners, extended the OLE DB interface to include data mining functionality. OLE DB for data mining describes the data mining process, which encompasses selecting data, creating models from a data sample, exploring those models, and (where the algorithms support it) using the models to form predictions.

To simplify data mining without lessening its power, data mining models can be created through a simple wizard in SQL Server. The user selects data (from a multidimensional cube or any OLE DB or ODBC data source) to use as the sample data. This sampling process trains the data mining model, resulting in a summary of knowledge about that data. The actual knowledge or insight gained depends on the algorithm the user selected. Microsoft ships the most common and widely applicable algorithms, and DWA (Microsoft Data Warehousing Alliance) members provide specialized algorithms attuned for particular markets and functions.

Once the data mining model is built and trained, it can be applied to new data to find anomalies and patterns and make predictions. The actual functionality at this point will depend on the algorithm that has been applied.

English Query

Query and reporting tools provide users with mechanisms for designing and distributing reports and building decision support systems and executive information systems. SQL Server provides all the features necessary to support these applications. In terms of languages, SQL uses the ANSI 1992 Standard

SQL; queries are posed to the relational engine (and other OLE DB data sources) in a standard way. Multidimensional Expression (MDX), a language developed by Microsoft and its partners specifically to query multidimensional data sources, allows users to define succinct queries that return powerful reports and analyses. And the built-in English Query facility translates English questions into SQL or MDX for querying relational or multidimensional stores.

English Query is a natural language interface that performs complex analyses of large data sets simply by asking questions in plain English. Users without an extensive background in SQL programming can use the power of SQL Server in freeform queries. Underlying this powerful translation engine is a semantic model that can be built automatically and extended for greater subject knowledge.

Meta Data Services

Microsoft SQL Server 2000 Meta Data Services is an object-oriented repository technology that can be integrated with enterprise information systems or with applications that process metadata.

A number of Microsoft technologies use Meta Data Services as a native store for object definitions or as a platform for deploying metadata. Meta Data Services can also be used as a component of an integrated information system, as a native store for custom applications that process metadata, or as a storage and management service for sharing reusable models.

Data Analyzer

Microsoft Data Analyzer is a member of the Office suite. It allows users to visualize data collected by their e-commerce, CRM, ERP, and other systems, which permits sophisticated data analysis by any business decision maker. Its main benefit is that it reduces an organization's dependence on analysts and increases the speed with which raw data becomes actionable information. Data Analyzer's value comes in allowing users to do the following:

- *Quickly analyze business data.* Visualization capabilities and graphical views enable users to identify opportunities and trends, find business anomalies, and review multiple sets of data in one interface for better decision making.

- *Improve data analysis productivity.* Options for displaying multiple measures, such as gross profit, unit sales, or quantity, or for displaying relationships between unlimited business dimensions, such as customer, region, or product, are available in a single, easy-to-use interface.

- *Easily publish and share business data.* Data Analyzer publishing and reporting capabilities make it easy to share data with others, access data analysis tools via the Web, and graphically publish data using other Office applications, such as Excel and Microsoft PowerPoint.

- *Find business data anomalies and trends automatically.* Guided analysis tools provide standardized questions for analyzing data; built-in template measures can easily identify KPIs; and filters can quickly select and filter certain criteria.

- *Leverage existing applications and computing environment.* With Data Analyzer, users can easily access data analysis tools over a network, over the Web, or in remote/offline scenarios. In addition to client/server access, Data Analyzer supports remote connection to OLAP cubes and the analysis of local cubes.

- *Integrate with enterprise BI tools.* Data Analyzer extends the BI capabilities of Microsoft Office XP by adding rich visualization and analysis capabilities. Data Analyzer's intuitive user interface and predefined queries complement the powerful analysis features provided by Excel 2002, Office Web Components, and digital dashboards.

Microsoft Data Analyzer is also designed to work with SQL Server Analysis Services 2000. Organizations that rely on SQL Server and SQL Server Analysis Services to collect and store business data in their enterprise systems can take advantage of Data Analyzer's guided analysis features by giving more users access to this information and existing analysts a new tool.

Microsoft Business Intelligence Accelerator

The newest piece of the Microsoft BI platform is the Microsoft Business Intelligence Accelerator for SQL Server, with multiple reference data models, including data models for sales and marketing analytics and retail analytics.

The Microsoft BI Accelerator is part of a larger effort at Microsoft to offer end-to-end solutions to customers. Microsoft solutions integrate products and technologies into targeted responses to customer problems and address business issues, as well as platform development, deployment, and management issues facing IT.

A Microsoft solution is differentiated from a traditional product-based approach in the level of integrated testing and documentation combined with prepackaged services and solution-level support. These offerings consist of existing Microsoft products, business application and integration code, and detailed architectural guidance. The benefit to customers is an end-to-end tested and documented solution.

The Microsoft BI Accelerator embodies a comprehensive set of best practices and supplies a mechanism to learn about and use best practices for constructing solidly built analytical applications using SQL Server 2000 and SQL Services Analysis Services 2000. The BI Accelerator is built on the foundation of the Microsoft Data Warehousing Framework.

The BI Accelerator has several components. The Analytics Builder Workbook is an Excel workbook in which you configure your data model, based on one of the reference data models, for example, sales and marketing analytics, retail analytics, or a third-party data model. The Analytics Builder utility then creates an analytical application based on the data model configured in the workbook.

Operational data flows into the analytical application, beginning with the Staging Database, which is a relational database temporarily storing new inserts and updates and occasionally deleting data from operational systems. DTS packages move data from the Staging Database into the Subject Matter Database, which is another relational database storing the cleansed and consolidated data. Through DTS packages, the Subject Matter Database then supplies BI data to the Analysis Database, a multidimensional database containing BI data in cubes, dimensions, and partitions. The Analysis Database is also where KPIs are exposed through collections of preconfigured client views for various business users and their needs. The BI Accelerator ships with preconfigured client views for the sales and marketing analytics data model and the retail analytics data model for Excel 2002, Microsoft Data Analyzer, and ProClarity Analytic Platform 4.0 clients. Client views for additional clients and additional data models are available from Microsoft and third-party Microsoft solution providers.

Prescriptive Architecture Guides from Microsoft provide extensive guidance to the BI architect for developing, deploying, operating, and maintaining the analytical application created by the Microsoft BI Accelerator. This guidance is based on real-world experience and is created and reviewed by Microsoft architects and development teams, Microsoft consultants, and Microsoft's internal IT group. The guidelines and best practices incorporated into these documents help assure consistent and successful results.

For continually updated information on the Microsoft BI Accelerator, please go to *www.microsoft.com/business/solutions*.

Data Warehousing Alliance

The Microsoft Data Warehousing Alliance (DWA) is a technical and marketing partnership between Microsoft and select independent software vendors focused on helping customers build, use, and manage data warehousing solutions that are fully integrated with SQL Server, Office, and the Microsoft Windows platform. DWA-member products extend the Microsoft platform through several means: extraction, transformation, and loading; analytical applications; query, reporting, and analysis; and data mining.

The Microsoft DWA offers customers a wide choice of tools to meet a variety of data analysis needs. And tight integration with Microsoft Office 2000 and Office XP means that users can perform sophisticated analyses on large data sets by using familiar tools. Users familiar with Office, especially Excel 2000 and Excel 2002, can obtain rich access to SQL Server 2000 data. Workers can create dynamic views of OLAP cubes using Microsoft PivotTable functionality. Excel 2000 and Excel 2002 also make it easy for any user to save a spreadsheet, chart, or PivotTable as a Web page, letting the user share that information with other people, who can then access and analyze the data.

For more information on members of Microsoft's Data Warehouse Alliance, see *www.microsoft.com*.

Glossary

80/20 rule   A theory invented by Vilfredo Pareto in the late 1800s, also known as the Pareto principle, that describes the percentage imbalance between input and output. The Pareto principle is not a law of science; rather, it is a rule of thumb that can apply to many aspects of life. One of the most common business examples is when 80 percent of a company's revenue comes from 20 percent of its customers.

actionability   A criterion used to grade the importance of a BI opportunity area based on its prospects of empowering people to take action in an organization. Actionability ratings are high, medium, and low.

ad hoc analysis   The impromptu and flexible examination of data without predefined or fixed formats. Ad hoc analysis gives users the ability to ask and get answers to an infinite variety of questions quickly.

affinity grouping   A descriptive data mining task that describes which items go together based on a set of characteristics.

alternate hierarchy   A different grouping of levels in a dimension. A dimension can have several alternate hierarchies to meet various analysis needs.

analysis gap   A gap between the information that decision makers require and the mountains of data that businesses collect every day.

ancestor   Any member of a dimension at any higher level in relation to another member of the same dimension.

base measure   A measure that is captured at the transaction level in an operational system.

benchmark   A measure used for making comparisons, for example, industry-specific ratios such as a price/earnings ratio.

BI   *See* business intelligence.

BI cycle   A performance management framework; an ongoing cycle by which companies set their goals, analyze their progress, gain insight, take action, measure their success, and start all over again.

BI solution   A mechanism that brings together people, technology, and data to deliver valuable information to business users.

blueprint   A table that documents the measures and dimensions for answering business questions and reflects the most fundamental requirements for building BI solutions.

business intelligence (BI)   An approach to management that allows an organization to define what information is useful and relevant to its corporate decision making. Business intelligence is a multifaceted concept that empowers organizations to make better decisions faster, convert data into information, and use a rational approach to management.

business reporting and analysis process   A subset of processes responsible for taking data from a BI system, such as a data warehouse, assembling it into a business-friendly format, and delivering data to business users.

business-to-business (B2B)   The exchange of products, services, or information between businesses.

business-to-consumer (B2C)   The exchange of products, services, or information between businesses and consumers.

business unit   An organizational structure in which a coherent set of functional activities rolls up into one line of business.

calculated measure   A measure that is calculated or derived from a combination of base measures.

child   A member that is directly subordinate to another member in a hierarchy.

classification   A predictive data mining task that assigns records to specific categories according to the rules of a data mining model.

click-stream analysis   The analysis of a user's interaction with a Web site by investigating the data that is generated with each user's click in a Web browser. The goal of click-stream analysis is to understand the behavior of Web site visitors, identify their likes and dislikes, and use this information to improve the quality of the Web site.

closed-loop analysis   A process that allows end users to act on the outcomes of their analyses to automatically drive business processes.

clustering   A descriptive data mining task that divides data into small groups based on similarity without predefinition of the data groups.

cube   A multidimensional data structure that represents the intersections of each unique combination of dimensions. At each intersection there is a cell that contains a data value.

custom aggregation   A method of summarizing data from its lowest level of detail to its highest level of detail in which measures are aggregated differently across different levels of a dimension.

database   A collection of related data that is organized in a useful manner for easy retrieval. There are different applications of databases depending on the type of data to be stored and how the data is to be used.

data modelers   Specialists who work with businesspeople and the technical experts during the implementation of a BI solution. Data modelers are responsible for gathering business requirements and translating these requirements into a realistic design of dimensions and measures.

data mining   An automated process that uses a variety of analysis tools and statistical techniques to reveal actionable patterns and relationships in large, complex data sets.

data mart   A collection of data that is structured in a way to facilitate analysis. Data marts support the study of a single subject area, with all relevant data from all operational applications brought together into that data mart. Data marts may be of the relational (RDBMS) variety or the OLAP variety depending on the type of analysis to be performed.

data warehouse   A repository for data. Many experts define the data warehouse as a centralized data store that feeds data into a series of subject-specific data stores—called data marts. Others accept a broader definition of the data warehouse as a collection of integrated data marts.

descendant   Any member at any lower level in relation to another specific member.

decision tree   A model for breaking data into groups. A decision tree uses a statistical algorithm to split the set of data being mined into branches of a tree.

descriptive data mining   A form of data mining that produces a model to describe patterns in historical data and requires human interaction to determine the significance and meaning of these patterns.

desktop online analytical processing (DOLAP)   An OLAP storage mode that keeps data on a client's machine and provides local multidimensional analysis.

dimension   A categorically consistent view of data. All members of a dimension belong together as a group.

dirty data   Data that is uncleansed or invalid because it is missing, incorrect, or duplicated.

DOLAP   *See* desktop online analytical processing (DOLAP).

EDI   *See* electronic data interchange (EDI).

electronic data interchange (EDI)   A standard for the electronic exchange of business data.

enterprise resource planning (ERP) system   A business management system that integrates all facets of the business, including planning, manufacturing, sales, and marketing. ERP systems are most often implemented using packaged software applications that support each facet of the business.

ERP system   *See* enterprise resource planning (ERP) system.

estimation   A predictive data mining task used to assign a new record with a predicted value according to the rules of a data mining model.

ETL   *See* extract, transform, and load (ETL) processes.

Extensible Markup Language for Analysis (XML/A)   A standard protocol that OLAP clients can use to talk to OLAP servers. XML/A is based on the widely adopted XML (Extensible Markup Language) standard and uses the programming language Multidimensional Expressions (MDX).

extract, transform, and load (ETL) processes   Processes that are responsible for transporting and integrating data from one or more source systems into one or more destination systems.

front-end tool   A category of software that harvests the data stored in a data warehouse and presents the data to users in the form of reports and interactive reviews.

functional area   A department of a business unit that is focused on a specific function.

hierarchy   The organization of levels within a dimension that (1) reflects how data is aggregated from detailed levels to summarized levels and (2) serves as the drill-down path for top-down business analysis.

HOLAP   *See* hybrid online analytical processing (HOLAP).

hybrid online analytical processing (HOLAP)   An OLAP tool that can store data in both multidimensional databases and relational databases.

information consumer   A community of business users that requires the ability to dynamically query the database via a "guided" user experience that allows drill down and pivoting when desired, while eliminating options that may create undesirable results.

information user   A community of business users that generally requires standard reports without needing to analyze the data on an ad hoc basis.

interoperability   A product's ability to work together and interact with other products.

key performance indicator (KPI)   A measure that ranks as one of the most important metrics in an organization. KPIs guide businesses in making decisions that affect particular business units as well as the company at large. *Key performance indicator* is used interchangeably with *metric*.

KPI   *See* key performance indicator (KPI).

leaf member   A bottom-level member in a dimension.

materiality   A criterion used to grade the importance of an BI opportunity area based on how financially significant the opportunity is to the organization. Materiality ratings are high, medium, and low.

measure   A numeric value that is of interest to business analysis.

member   An item in a dimension that represents one or more occurrences of data.

mental model   A collection of everything that we think we know about how something works (in this case our business). This labeling of our understanding applies to not only people but also organizations. Some people refer to the company's mental model as "tribal wisdom."

metadata   Information about the properties of data, such as business logic that describes the structure and content of dimensions and measures.

metric   A measure that guides businesses in making decisions that affect particular business units as well as the company at large. *Metric* is used interchangeably with *key performance indicator*.

MOLAP   *See* multidimensional online analytical processing (MOLAP).

multidimensional analysis   A way of analyzing data in a top-down fashion by examining measures simultaneously broken out by multiple dimensions.

multidimensional online analytical processing (MOLAP)   An OLAP storage mode in which data is placed into special structures that are stored on a central server(s).

OLAP   *See* online analytical processing (OLAP).

OLE DB   An application programming interface (API) for accessing data. OLE DB supports accessing data stored in any format (databases, spreadsheets, text files, and so on) for which an OLE DB provider is available.

OLE DB for OLAP   Formerly the separate specification that addressed OLAP extensions to OLE DB. Beginning with OLE DB 2.0, OLAP extensions are incorporated into the OLE DB specification.

OLTP   *See* online transaction processing (OLTP).

online analytical processing (OLAP)   Multidimensional analysis that is supported by interface tools and database structures that allow instantaneous access and easy user manipulation. Online analytical processing got its name because this name contrasts well with OLTP, a term that was already in widespread use when the term OLAP was created. There are fundamental differences between transaction processing and analytical processing. OLAP systems support multidimensional analysis at the speed of thought. OLAP typically follows the client/server paradigm, where an OLAP database *server* is accessed by many users who use multidimensional *client* tools to analyze data.

online transaction processing (OLTP)   A data processing system designed to record all the business transactions of an organization as they occur. OLTP systems are structured for the purposes of running the day-to-day raw data of business, which requires efficiency and minute processing of transactions at the lowest level of detail. An OLTP system processes a transaction, performs all the elements of the transaction in real time, and processes many transactions on a continuous basis. OLTP systems usually offer little or no analytical capabilities.

open database connectivity (ODBC)   A data access application programming interface (API) that supports access to any data source for which an ODBC driver is available. ODBC is aligned with the American National Standards Institute (ANSI) and International Organization for Standardization (ISO) standards for a database call level interface (CLI).

operational database   A database that supports the day-to-day operations of an organization. Operational databases host the systems that organizations use to run their business day to day. Most operational databases are OLTP systems and store the data in a relational database management system.

opportunity area   In BI technical terms, the logical grouping of measure requirements, where data can be obtained consistently across all the dimensions at the same lowest level of detail. In business terms, similar to a project where a consistent set of requirements for a group of users can be accommodated more or less from the same end-to-end system structures or solution.

parent   A member that is directly above another member in a hierarchy.

pilot project   A short-term BI project that tests the feasibility of pursuing a specific opportunity area.

pivot and nest   Point-and-click manipulations that facilitate multidimensional analysis. Pivoting means rotating rows to columns, and columns to rows, in a cross-tabular data browser. Nesting is layering multiple dimensions on the rows or columns of a browser.

power analyst   A community of business users that requires the full analytical power of the data mart. These users are willing to learn the details of database design and the query tool in order to obtain the necessary results.

predictive data mining   Data mining that produces a model for use with new data to forecast a value or predict a probable outcome based on patterns discovered in historical data.

proof-of-concept project   A BI project that evaluates and selects technologies that can be used to host a data mart.

ragged hierarchy   A hierarchy that has an inconsistent number of drill-down levels.

ratio   A measure where the result is calculated specifically from dividing one measure by another.

RDBMS   *See* relational database management system (RDBMS).

refresh rate   The frequency by which data is updated. Typically the refresh rate corresponds to the lowest level of detail of a time dimension required for a group of measures.

relational database management system (RDBMS)   A set of programs that allows users to create, update, and administer data that is stored in a database of related tables.

relational online analytical processing (ROLAP)   An OLAP storage mode where data is stored in relational databases.

ROLAP   *See* relational online analytical processing (ROLAP).

roll-up   The hierarchical aggregations of data typical in multidimensional structures.

segmentation   A data mining technique that analyzes data to discover mutually exclusive collections of records that share similar attribute sets. A segmentation algorithm can use unsupervised learning techniques such as clustering or supervised learning for a specific prediction field.

semiadditive aggregation   A method of summarizing data from its lowest level of detail to its highest level of detail in which measures are not aggregated uniformly across all dimensions.

sibling   A member that is at the same level as one or more other members sharing the same parent.

slice and dice   Two complementary methods for interacting with data. Slicing means isolating a specific member of a dimension for analysis. Dicing means breaking a data set into smaller pieces by examining how measures intersect with multiple dimensions.

slowly changing dimension   A term that describes how dimensions reflect data changes over time.

SQL   *See* structured query language (SQL).

structured query language (SQL; pronounced *sequel*)   An industry standard language for accessing data (also called querying) in a relational database management system (RDBMS).

uniform aggregation   A method of summarizing data from its lowest level of detail to its highest level of detail, where data can be aggregated the same way across all dimensions.

visualization   A graphical representation of data that sometimes reveals patterns that are more apparent to the human eye.

write back   The ability for users to update data in an underlying data mart.

zero client footprint   A tool that does not require software to be installed on a business user's desktop, thus making the client application easier to deploy to more users.

Bibliography

Berry, Michael J. A., and Gordon Linoff. 2000. *Mastering data mining: The art and science of customer relationship management.* New York: John Wiley & Sons, Inc.

Connelly, Richard, Robin McNeill, and Roland Mosimann. 1996. *The multidimensional manager: 24 ways to impact your bottom line in 90 days.* Ottawa, Ont., Canada: Cognos Incorporated.

de Ville, Barry. 2001. *Microsoft data mining: Integrated business intelligence for e-commerce and knowledge management.* Woburn, Mass.: Butterworth-Heinemann.

Dresner, Howard. 2001. *Business intelligence: Making the data make sense.* Paper presented at Gartner Group U.S. Spring Symposium/ITxpo 2001, 7–10 May, Denver, Colo. Copyrighted by Gartner Group, Inc., Stamford, Conn.

Imhoff, Claudia, Lisa Loftis, and Jonathan G. Geiger. 2001. *Building the customer-centric enterprise: Data warehousing techniques for supporting customer relationship management.* New York: John Wiley & Sons, Inc.

Kimball, Ralph. 1996. *The data warehouse toolkit: Practical techniques for building dimensional data warehouses.* New York: John Wiley & Sons, Inc.

Kimball, Ralph, Laura Reeves, Margy Ross, and Warren Thornthwaite. 1998. *The data warehouse lifecycle toolkit: Expert methods for designing, developing, and deploying data warehouses.* New York: John Wiley & Sons, Inc.

Kuhn, Thomas S. 1962. *The structure of scientific revolutions.* Chicago: University of Chicago Press.

Liautaud, Bernard, and Mark Hammond. 2001. *E-business intelligence: Turning information into knowledge into profit.* New York: McGraw-Hill, Inc.

OLAP Train, and Reed Jacobson. 2000. *The Microsoft SQL Server 2000 Analysis Services step by step.* Redmond, Wash.: Microsoft Press.

Peters, Thomas J., and Robert H. Waterman, Jr. 1982. *In search of excellence.* New York: Harper & Row.

Pendse, Nigel. *The OLAP report.* This report is available online at http://www.olapreport.com.

Senge, Peter M. 1994. *The fifth discipline: The art and practice of the learning organization.* New York: Doubleday.

Tufte, Edward R. 1983. *The visual display of quantitative information.* Cheshire, Conn.: Graphics Press.

Index

The manuscript for this book was prepared and galleyed using Microsoft Word Version 2002. Pages were composed by Black Dot Group/An AGT Company using QuarkXPress for Macintosh, with text and display type in ITC Clearface. Composed pages were delivered to the printer as electronic prepress files.

Cover designer:	Hornall Anderson Design Works
Interior Graphic Designer:	Joel Panchot
Interior Graphic Artist:	Black Dot Group/An AGT Company
Principal Compositor:	Black Dot Group/An AGT Company
Principal Proofreader:	Black Dot Group/An AGT Company
Indexer:	Black Dot Group/An AGT Company

Learning solutions for *every* software user

Microsoft Press learning solutions are ideal for every software user— from business users to developers to IT professionals

Microsoft Press® creates comprehensive learning solutions that empower everyone from business professionals and decision makers to software developers and IT professionals to work more productively with Microsoft® software. We design books for every business computer user, from beginners up to tech-savvy power users. We produce in-depth learning and reference titles to help developers work more productively with Microsoft programming tools and technologies. And we give IT professionals the training and technical resources they need to deploy, install, and support Microsoft products during all phases of the software adoption cycle. Whatever technology you're working with and no matter what your skill level, we have a learning tool to help you.

Microsoft®
microsoft.com/mspress

Discover how to meet
mission-critical
business needs
with customizable technology solutions!

In today's changing business environment, your success depends on knowing how to stay ahead of the competition. Microsoft and its partners have worked closely with hundreds of business decision-makers to create custom solutions designed to help you get ahead and stay there. These solutions integrate leading technologies, applications, and services into packages tailored to meet mission-critical business needs. A new line of books from Microsoft describes in detail how these solutions can help you speed your time to market and solve your pressing business needs—complete with real-life examples of solutions in action.

Business Intelligence
>*Making Better Decisions Faster*
U.S.A.   **$39.99**
Canada $57.99
ISBN: 0-7356-1627-2

Supplier Empowerment
>*Solutions for Business-to-Business E-Commerce*
U.S.A.   **$39.99**
Canada $57.99
ISBN: 0-7356-1627-2

Collective Knowledge
>*Intranets, Productivity, and the Promise of the Knowledge Workplace*
U.S.A.   **$39.99**
Canada $57.99
ISBN: 0-7356-1499-7

Connecting to Customers
>*Strategies and Solutions for Growing Your Business Online*
U.S.A.   **$39.99**
Canada $57.99
ISBN: 0-7356-1500-4

HIPAA Compliance Solutions
>*Comprehensive Strategies from Microsoft and Washington Publishing Company*
U.S.A.   **$39.99**
Canada $57.99
ISBN: 0-7356-1496-2

Microsoft Press® products are available worldwide wherever quality computer books are sold. For more information, contact your book or computer retailer, software reseller, or local Microsoft® Sales Office, or visit our Web site at microsoft.com/mspress. To locate your nearest source for Microsoft Press products, or to order directly, call 1-800-MSPRESS in the United States (in Canada, call 1-800-268-2222).

Prices and availability dates are subject to change.

Microsoft®
microsoft.com/mspress

Get a **Free**

e-mail newsletter, updates,
special offers, links to related books,
and more when you

register on line!

Register your Microsoft Press® title on our Web site and you'll get
a FREE subscription to our e-mail newsletter, *Microsoft Press Book
Connections.* You'll find out about newly released and upcoming books
and learning tools, online events, software downloads, special offers
and coupons for Microsoft Press customers, and information about
major Microsoft® product releases. You can also read useful additional
information about all the titles we publish, such as detailed book descriptions, tables of contents and indexes, sample chapters, links to
related books and book series, author biographies, and reviews by
other customers.

Registration is easy. Just visit this Web page and fill in your information:

http://www.microsoft.com/mspress/register

Microsoft®
